Library of
Davidson College

BRICK ARCHITECTURE OF THE COLONIAL PERIOD
IN MARYLAND & VIRGINIA

BY

Lewis A. Coffin Jr. &
Arthur C. Holden

DOVER PUBLICATIONS, INC
NEW YORK

Copyright © 1970 by Dover Publications, Inc.
All rights reserved under Pan American and International Copyright Conventions.

This Dover edition, first published in 1970, is an unabridged republication of the work originally published by Architectural Book Publishing Co. in 1919. A list of plates has been prepared for this reprint edition.

International Standard Book Number: 0-486-22488-0
Library of Congress Catalog Card Number: 73-125625

Manufactured in the United States of America
Dover Publications, Inc.
180 Varick Street
New York, N. Y. 10014

LIST OF PLATES
Maryland

BRICE HOUSE, ANNAPOLIS
PLATES
1 Front view
2 Front elevation (drawing)
3 Exterior details (drawing)
4 Mantel in living room
5 Mantel in living room (drawing)
6 Living room plan (drawing)
7 Mantel in parlor (drawing)
8 Mantel in dining room (drawing)
9 Details of carved mantels

HARWOOD HOUSE, ANNAPOLIS
10 Entrance doorway
11 Entrance doorway (drawing)
12 Garden elevation

CHASE HOUSE, ANNAPOLIS
13 Entrance doorway
14 (*left*) Rear, showing stair window
14 (*right*) Interior detail, dining room
15 Palladian window (drawing)
16 Window detail (drawing)
17 Interior doorways (drawing)
18 Mantel piece (drawing)

RIDOUT HOUSE, ANNAPOLIS
19 (*top*) Garden elevation

CARVEL HOUSE, ANNAPOLIS
19 (*bottom*) Garden elevation
20 (*top*) Entrance hall and stair

ACTON, ANNAPOLIS
20 (*bottom*) Front view
21 Front elevation and detail of main cornice (drawing)

WHITEHALL, ANNE ARUNDEL COUNTY
22 Front view
23 (*top*) View from the old garden
23 (*bottom*) Detail from the west wing
24 Rear View
25 Exterior window and interior door (drawing)
26 Detail of parlor and dining room mantel, and interior door (drawing)
27 (*top*) Interior of saloon

TULIP HILL, ANNE ARUNDEL COUNTY
27 (*bottom*) Front view
28 Elevation of the terraces and canopy (drawing)
29 (*top*) View from terraces
29 (*bottom*) Staircase
30 Entrance Hall
31 Details of stairway (drawing)

RATCLIFFE MANOR, TALBOT COUNTY
32 (*top*) Front view
32 (*bottom*) View from the garden

HOMEWOOD, BALTIMORE COUNTY
33 Front view
34 Entrance porch

LIST OF PLATES

HOUSES IN ST. MARY'S COUNTY
35 (*top, left*) Front view of Mulberry Fields
35 (*top, right*) Front and side view of house
35 (*bottom, left*) Front view of house
35 (*bottom, right*) Front view of Francis Scott Key House
36 (*top*) Interior living room, farmhouse
36 (*bottom*) Side view of house

Virginia

WOODLAWN, FAIRFAX COUNTY
37 (*top*) View before rebuilding
37 (*bottom*) View of the river side
38 (*top*) Staircase

GUNSTON HALL, FAIRFAX COUNTY
38 (*bottom*) View from the garden
39 Front view
40 (*top*) Entrance hall and stairs
40 (*bottom*) Drawing room

CHRIST CHURCH, ALEXANDRIA
41 Christ Church
42 Doorway (drawing)
43 (*top*) Interior

POHICK PARISH CHURCH, FAIRFAX COUNTY
43 (*bottom*) Front view
44 Doorway (drawing)

LLOYD HOUSE, ALEXANDRIA
45 Doorway

HOUSES IN FREDERICKSBURG
46 (*top*) View of doorway
46 (*bottom*) View of doorway

MUNDY HOUSE, DUMPHRIES
47 Mantel piece (drawing)
48 (*top*) Drawing room

HOUSE ON MAIN STREET, FREDERICKSBURG
48 (*bottom*) Front view

KENMORE, FREDERICKSBURG
49 (*top*) Front view
49 (*bottom*) Staircase
50 Mantel in saloon and parlor
51 Ceiling in parlor
52 (*top*) Ceiling in saloon
52 (*bottom*) Ceiling in dining room

STRATFORD, WESTMORELAND COUNTY
53 Front view

CLEVE MANOR, KING GEORGE COUNTY
54 (*top*) Front view

GAY MOUNT, CAROLINE COUNTY
54 (*bottom*) Front and side view

BROCKENBOROUGH HOUSE, ESSEX COUNTY
55 Front View

BLANDFIELD, ESSEX COUNTY
56 (*top*) Front view

BROOKS BANK, ESSEX COUNTY
56 (*bottom*) Front view

LIST OF PLATES

SABINE HALL, RICHMOND COUNTY
57 Front view
58 Front view (drawing)
59 Stairway from the main hall

MOUNT AIRY, RICHMOND COUNTY
60 East front
61 River front
62 Detail of front view, entrance portico and pilaster (drawing)
63 (*left*) Carved urns
63 (*right*) Detail of south window
64 Garden motive and entrance court (drawing)

MENOKIN, RICHMOND COUNTY
65 (*left*) Living room
65 (*right*) Stair hall

BRUTON PARISH CHURCH, WILLIAMSBURG
66 Front view
67 Transept door
68 Front view with details (drawing)
69 (*top*) Front view

THE COURT HOUSE, WILLIAMSBURG
69 (*bottom*) Front and side view
70 Front elevation with detail of cornice and side elevation (drawing)

WHYTHE HOUSE, WILLIAMSBURG
71 (*top*) Front view

SAUNDERS HOUSE, WILLIAMSBURG
71 Front and side view

BASSET HALL, WILLIAMSBURG
72 (*top*) Front view

MALVERN HOUSE, HENRICO COUNTY
72 (*bottom*) Front view

CARTERS'S GROVE, JAMES CITY COUNTY
73 East front
74 Entrance hall
75 (*left*) Stair detail
75 (*right*) Doorway to parlor
76 Elevations of south-west room (drawing)
77 Details of south-west room (drawing)

SHIRLEY, CHARLES CITY COUNTY
78 View from the garden
79 East porch
80 Two-story porch (drawing)
81 (*left*) Stair landing
81 (*right*) "Hanging Stair" and hall
82 Mantel and details of hall (drawing)
83 The saloon
84 Mantel piece (drawing)
85 Mantel piece, chair-rail, etc. (drawing)
86 Interior doorway (drawing)
87 Detail from parlor
88 Detail from dining room
89 Interior doorway (drawing)
90 (*top*) Old dovecote
90 (*bottom*) Farm buildings facing office

WESTOVER, CHARLES CITY COUNTY
91 Front view
92 (*top*) Doorway
92 (*bottom*) Gate and main gate
93 (*top*) Entrance hall
93 (*bottom*) Detail of stairway

LOWER BRANDON, PRINCE GEORGE COUNTY
94 View from the river side

LIST OF PLATES

95 (*top*) Entrance hall
95 (*bottom*) Parlor
96 (*top*) Garden

BACON'S CASTLE, SURRY COUNTY
96 (*bottom*) Side view

MOUNT VERNON, FAIRFAX COUNTY
97 (*top*) Front view

NELSON HOUSE, YORK COUNTY
97 (*bottom*) Front view

OLD HOUSE IN YORKTOWN
98 Front and side view

ROSEWELL, GLOUCESTER COUNTY
99 (*top*) Front and side view
99 (*bottom*) Grand staircase

WILTON, HENRICO COUNTY
100 (*top*) View from the river side

ABINGTON CHURCH, GLOUCESTER COUNTY
100 (*bottom*) Front and side view

WILTON, HENRICO COUNTY
101 (*left*) Staircase
101 (*right*) West door

TUCKAHOE, GOOCHLAND COUNTY
102 Box garden
103 (*top*) Front and side view
103 (*bottom*) South stairs
104 (*top*) Mantel in northeast room
104 (*bottom*) North stairs
105 Carved ornament, risers and newel of north stairs

MYERS HOUSE, NORFOLK
106 Corner view
107 (*top*) Library
107 (*bottom*) Mantel in parlor

MONTPELIER, ORANGE COUNTY
108 Front view (showing reconstructed wings)
109 Giant box
110 (*top*) Garden
110 (*bottom*) Garden from the upper terrace

ESTOUTEVILLE, ALBERMARLE COUNTY
111 Front view

COURT HOUSE, GOOCHLAND COUNTY
112 (*top*) Front and side view

THE ROTUNDA, CHARLOTTESVILLE
112 (*bottom*) Front view
113 Front view of Rotunda and Quadrangle

MONTICELLO, ALBERMARLE COUNTY
114 South portico
115 (*top*) North portico
115 (*bottom*) West wing
116 (*top*) Main hall
116 (*bottom*) Reception room

FARMINGTON, ALBERMARLE COUNTY
117 (*top*) Front view

TALLWOOD, ALBERMARLE COUNTY
117 (*bottom*) Mantel in parlor

BREMO, FLUVANNA COUNTY
118 (*top*) Front view
118 (*bottom*) View from the river side

BRICK ARCHITECTURE
OF THE COLONIAL PERIOD
IN MARYLAND & VIRGINIA

INTRODUCTION

IN presenting a volume such as this of photographs and measured drawings, purporting to cover such a wide field as the Colonial Architecture of Maryland and Virginia, some words of explanation, perhaps of apology, are fitting. There were many difficulties encountered in procuring the photographs and data contained herein. Firstly, the buildings are widely scattered over two states, almost invariably at a distance from convenient transportation, even the roads being sometimes well-nigh impassable. Therefore, it was often difficult to devote a proper amount of time to obtaining the desirable data of the building visited. Then in a few unfortunate instances permission to take photographs was not by any means obtainable, and more often it was impossible to obtain measurements. A most hearty tribute is due to the hospitality of the owners of the majority of houses visited and to their understanding and help in the purpose of the work.

Whereas, the early architecture of New England, and the neighborhoods of New York, Philadelphia, and Washington, has been often and ably published, there has been for many years no serious attempt to cover the rich field for inquiry and study in Maryland and Virginia. There is no doubt of the importance to modern Colonial architecture of these old tidewater buildings, for they represent the Colonial architecture of brick in contrast to the less pretentious frame buildings of the north. The homes of Maryland and Virginia remain for us as the aristocrats of our early architecture, the forefathers of the modern brick Colonial style.

Rightness in this American style can best be helped and arrived at by the close friendship with these grand old prototypes, by the ready absorption of their essentials and a close study of their details. Unfortunately it is too often a fact that any red brick house with white wood work is termed Colonial, an unflattering commentary upon the knowledge and the taste of the public and the architect alike.

The Colonial houses of Maryland, still standing today, are scattered along the navigable rivers of the state and through those counties which border on Chesapeake Bay. It is therefore around the city of Baltimore, along the Severn, the West and the Patuxent Rivers and throughout the peninsula between the Chesapeake and the Potomac Rivers that most of the buildings of interest are to be found. The Eastern shore of Maryland, that strip of land between Chesapeake Bay and the Atlantic also contains several old places of great interest.

Annapolis, the capital of Maryland and one-time center of wealth and culture, contains the largest collection of good architectural examples, the town itself still retaining much of its ancient

INTRODUCTION

aspect and atmosphere. Originally the properties surrounding the important houses were extensive, in many cases reaching to the shore of the Bay or the Severn River, and almost invariably including wide orchards and gardens. Since that early time, however, the town has grown up around and in between the original homes, invading their orchards and infringing upon the gardens, until, as they stand to-day they seem too crowded together. Still, however, some evidences of the gardens remain, most frequently a half-obliterated terrace or walk of gigantic English boxwood.

These town houses of Annapolis are particularly noteworthy for the refinement and the elaboration of the wood detail, both on the exterior and interior. More richly carven wood detail than that in the Brice House and the Chase House would be difficult to find. This elaborateness and refinement reflect the wealth and tastes of the community that formed Annapolis in its days of glory. Indeed there is a semblance of decadence in some of the most ornate interiors, notably in those of the Brice House.

The brickwork is most interesting from many points and of great import to an architect. The color of the brick approximates a dull salmon and is distinctly different from brick-color found anywhere else in the country. It is very agreeable to the eye, giving a refreshing and not too glaring contrast with white trims and cornice. Larger in size than any used in modern work, averaging three by four by nine inches, the bricks are even and smooth in texture. The jointing employed is also uncommon, being seldom as much as one quarter inch, struck with a fine tool. The cement is a clean white in color, being made of white sand, and pulverized sea-shells, which supplied oftentimes the lime for the mixture. When the brick was laid, the joint seems to have bulged slightly and then to have been carefully struck, making a clean straight line about one-sixteenth of an inch wide on the face of the bulge. The effect of this fine line on a narrow white joint gives an added crispness and refinement to the brickwork. There are several bondings used, though the Flemish bond is by all odds the most commonly employed. All the work has been executed with great care and exactness, the bonding conforming with openings, and the courses of brick with the sills and heads of windows. Above doors and windows, flat arches of a slightly pinker and lighter colored brick serve both for a constructional and decorative effect. The jointing in these rubbed brick arches are practically nil, the brick being so hard and so carefully rubbed to size that they are unnecessary. A most interesting and effective bond, not often seen, is that of the Brice House street façade, the bonding throughout being all headers, breaking joints. Other examples of this bond are the Ridout House, the Carvel House in Annapolis and Mulberry Fields in St. Mary's County. However, it is often to be seen in the belt course of brick on a front elsewhere laid up in a Flemish bond.

Very high ceilings are common, thirteen feet being most usual on the first floor and slightly

INTRODUCTION

less on the second floor. Interior shutters, folding back into recesses at the sides of the window are usual, thereby obviating the necessity of exterior shutters. The height of ceilings and the absence of exterior shutters create the wide expanses of plain wall surfaces, so often lost in modern work, while the plainness of the openings with flush white trim emphasize the proportions of fenestration.

One of the most striking features of all Maryland Colonial houses is the great height and boldness of proportion of the chimneys. They have been made distinctly important features of the composition, lending a part in the character of façade of this old work. Those of the Brice House and the Ridout House, so wide on their sides, so thin and so daringly high above the ridge are particularly noteworthy, as well as the pierced and vaulted chimneys of Tulip Hill. Almost without exception chimneys on gable ends rise flush with the building wall, as no moulds along the rake are allowed to break the uninterrupted wall surface.

Among the houses outlying Annapolis is Whitehall which deserves a special mention for a most beautiful setting, a charming composition and the delicate carved interior details of mantels, doors and window trim. This carving, it is said, was executed by a prisoner of the Revolutionary War as a thank-offering for the kind treatment accorded him at Whitehall.

St. Mary's County, the earliest settled part of Maryland, abounds in old houses, less pretentious than those in Annapolis or tidewater Virginia, but none the less of considerable interest for their setting, composition or the originality of their lines. However, being of a very early date of construction and simple in design, there are only occasional details of interest. Across the Bay lies the Eastern Shore of Maryland, also settled in the early days and containing numerous examples of Colonial architecture worthy of note. At Ratcliffe Manor the magnificent approach through an avenue of trees nearly a mile in length, the house of dignified proportion with some excellent interior details and the extensive box garden leading to the water, are particularly interesting. At Wye the unusually well preserved garden is even more noteworthy, if the house is less so. The towns of Oxford and Cambridge contain some interesting relics of brick houses, while there are fine old homes less famous than those mentioned scattered along this Eastern Shore of Maryland.

The character of the Colonial style throughout Maryland seems to depend largely on these several factors: the most perfect proportion, the absence of exterior shutters and the consequent plain wall surface, the flush trim and heavy muntins of windows, the bold height of chimneys and the smooth gable ends on which the cornice does not return nor mouldings trim along the rakes, as well as the character of the brickwork and the refinement of jointing. There is an excellent composition in almost every building, a refinement of detail both interior and exterior, and a perfec-

INTRODUCTION

tion in scale, a certain boldness and at the same time a feeling of reserve, that gives to the architecture a superb dignity.

As in Maryland, Colonial Virginia grew up along the Chesapeake, its inlets and rivers and the tributaries thereto. It is almost a fruitless search for Colonial buildings in the inland districts away from water transportation, so all important was that factor to the early settlers. It was along the water-lands, the tidewater section of Virginia that the early estates were granted and later subdivided into smaller estates, along the banks of the James, the Rappahannock, the Potomac, and the York Rivers. It would be easy and fitting altogether to classify the homes of early Virginia in regard to the river on whose banks they stand, for so these Virginians themselves think of them, grouping themselves by both county limits and river-valley.

The old tidewater plantations represent the homes of transplanted English aristocracy, of chevalier families who brought with them their cultured European tastes and habits of life. With the advent of bonded slaves and later the negroes, they established what amounted to a veritable feudal system on large grants of land by the throne of England. This is well to be understood if the true atmosphere of these old plantations is to be grasped and indeed if the wherefore and the why of their homes is to be realized. Pride of family, pride of home, pride of country, has always been proverbial of Virginia and this pride has reflected itself in the resultant architecture, these old great monarchs of brick that still gaze out over half obliterated gardens, terraces falling away to the river shore and seemingly endless rolling acres of plantation land. It shows itself as well in the family grave-yard, closed in with a crumbling brick wall, half hidden behind cypress and yew and quite overgrown with old ivy, where the flat horizontal grave-stones have been carved with the family coat-of-arms. Likewise to understand their life is to understand the planning of the houses, the grouping and lay-out of out-buildings for kitchen, storehouses, slave quarters and the like, as well as the monumental scale of terraces and garden.

It is easy to dwell too long upon the atmosphere of old-world ease and refinement, and the faded glory that surrounds these plantations. It is a little difficult not to feel a resentment against a world which has swept on ruthlessly, leaving that early civilization to struggle with war and poverty, and to die.

The approach from the main high-road to many of the old places is often a monumental scheme, a straight avenue of trees seventy or a hundred feet wide, whose branches almost form a roof overhead, and between which afar off, the house with its white doorway or porch forms the terminal feature. These grand approaches are more common in Maryland than Virginia.

The gardens, planned usually on the main axis of the house, lie on the other side from the approach, that is towards the water front. With some exceptions they have felt the hand of time

INTRODUCTION

more heavily than the houses, and of many of them little remains other than a gigantic untrimmed boxwood walk. Everyone is familiar with the part boxwood played in these old gardens, bordering the walks, enclosing the rose garden or hedging in the lawn. Sometimes a large clump of box or the box walk supplies the main feature of a garden. At Tuckahoe on the upper James, there is a most interesting and effective labyrinthine garden of box trimmed walks, enclosing the plots for flowers. The use of trees to form avenues of approach, to limit the spread of lawn and garden is interesting: a suggestion to landscape architects who desire to plan for a long future. For the trees now majestically tall, create an effect of beauty and dignity that no other means can approach. At Sabine Hall on the Rappahannock, the feature of the flower garden is an ancient and towering oak. Many of the larger gardens are truly monumental in scale such as Lower Brandon on the James, Mt. Airy on the Rappahannock and Montpelier in Orange County.

The typical plan of the houses is a five part composition, a central, two connecting and two end wings. Occasionally the connecting wings have been omitted as in Carter's Grove. The two end buildings being so placed and of such a size that together with the central Building, a well tied-together composition is formed. In general the central house, contains the living quarters of the family. The first floor is almost invariably planned with wide central hall, a graceful stairway, with the remaining spaces forming four variously proportioned rooms. One room served for the dining room to which the food was carried from the kitchen in the connecting wing or oftentimes in an out building. The other three rooms were parlors, the living room or offices. On the second floor, the arrangement of space is often the same, the great central hall carrying through from front to rear. Almost without exception the rooms have fireplaces, one interior chimney taking care of four fireplaces, or in a four chimneyed building the fireplaces are on the exterior walls, two to each chimney. The end buildings served for kitchen, slaves' quarters or the home of the overseer and his family. The slaves were often housed in other out-buildings around the barns or in frame cottages throughout the plantation.

One of the most striking effects to an architect about the interiors is the dignity and charm of proportion of the rooms themselves, the unusualness and freshness of these proportions. This is somewhat due no doubt to the extraordinary ceiling heights, but is to a large extent the result of unconventionalized and well studied proportion. The detail of the woodwork in Virginia Colonial is bolder than that in Maryland, approaching sometimes in interior work to heaviness and even coarseness. But it is never without an abundant vigor, freshness and strength. Some of the interior detail has the scale of exterior work, while it may be said that the exterior detail is quite unexceptionally of excellent scale and quality. There are many shining examples of most refined interior woodwork however, such as Shirley, Westover, Tuckahoe and Lower Brandon, all on the James River. No more beautiful Colonial detail with all its crispness, strict scale and refinement can be found anywhere on the continent. As a rule the woodwork is sim-

INTRODUCTION

ple, not as rich in ornamentation as in Annapolis houses. The ornament employed, usually dentils, frets, egg and dart motive and some few more original has been used sparingly, but with the consequent supreme effect. A rather interesting feature is to be noted where the window trim sweeps out in a cavetto curve to meet the chair rail, as occurs in several examples. More appreciation of the difficulties the builders of these interiors were under, is had when it is realized that all mouldings were hewn, and run by hand and hand-made nails were used, wherever mortice and tenon methods could not better be employed. The paneling of wainscot and wall or firebreast is usually bold in scale of detail, almost invariably a raised paneling with small ovolo and cavetto mould trimming along the stiles, which are about three and a half to four inches in width. Stairways are interesting without exception, both for plan and detail, in the larger houses furnishing the most important feature of the interior. At Shirley there is a curious hanging stairway, unique in construction though not particularly pleasing to the eye. In several instances a straight run on the axis of the hall leads to a wide landing with stair window above, with a double return to the hall above. The newels and balusters are usually elaborate in design, fluted straight or spirally and the well-string richly carved with running floral ornament. Circular and elliptic stairways are not uncommon, in the smaller houses having been much used to accomplish the rise within a remarkably small space, the curve being both economical of space and graceful of line.

It probably always will remain a question as to by what men and by what means these early buildings were planned. Some surely are the work of English architects, such as Mt. Airy which is completely Georgian in all characteristics and the College of William and Mary, undoubtedly the design of Sir Christopher Wren. It is highly probable for many reasons, however, that the majority of the work is the result of the owners' or builders' ability and application to books. Undoubtedly books of English and Italian architecture they had, and it was by their clever and somewhat daring adaptation that the style of Colonial was born.

Large size bricks were employed in Virginia, laid in an almost invariably Flemish bond with belt course of some half-inch projection and light colored flat window arches. The jointing is often the same as in Annapolis houses, a narrow struck joint of white cement. The bricks are of a fine even quality and a glorious rich color now somewhat subdued and made motley with age. Much of the brick is supposed to have been brought from England as ballast for ships, but this seems unlikely when it is considered that cargo space was valuable and that there is an abundant supply of fine clay. There are a few examples of moulded brickwork, where a cavetto and ovolo moulded brick course forms the base mould for a building or more elaborately where the doorways are made, architrave, frieze and pediment with moulded brick. The several small parish churches erected by Queen Anne have these moulded brick bases and doorways, as well as Rosewell and Carter's Grove. Another feature of brickwork quite often encountered is the burnt glazed header in a Flemish bond, producing the diagonal pattern. This pattern often

INTRODUCTION

seems too rigid and glaring, but on the walls of old Bruton Parish Church gives a most splendid effect. It is a pity that photographs display none of the glory of color of this old brickwork, for with the vines that often half cover the walls, much of the beauty is in the coloring. The chimneys, as in Maryland houses, are almost without exception remarkable for bold height, becoming thereby important features of the composition.

Williamsburg is a center of great interest for the searcher after Colonial architecture. The small brick or white frame houses set back behind their gardens and white picket fences, contain excellent interiors, paneling, doorways and stairways. Originally the town was planned on a monumental scheme, the main avenue terminated at one end by William and Mary College and at the other by the Capitol and Capitol Square, though this later building has long since been destroyed by fire. The Court House, reputed to Wren, is still standing however, though restored after fire from the cornice upwards. The crowning feature, however, of Williamsburg is Old Bruton Parish Church, whose white tower rises above an ancient graveyard, the whole mellowed with age and half covered with vine. It is a building of supreme beauty, the color of its brick walls laid up in a Flemish bond with glazed headers, the white blinds and fat muntins, the rare colored vines clambering up the walls and along the perfect cornice, giving an effect in Colonial unsurpassed.

Around Charlottesville the architecture takes of an entirely different character from that of tide-water Virginia. This is due to the hand of Thomas Jefferson, much of the work was his own and the remainder built under his direct influence. The University of Virginia, Monticello the home of Jefferson, and indeed all the brick houses of that date and neighborhood bear the Jeffersonian print. Jefferson's original designs for the University drawn by his own hand, are still preserved in the University Library. An examination of them shows the care with which he copied and adapted the classic temples of Rome. His designs show also that he was a believer in almost mathematically balanced proportions and all dimensions are given in terms of modules and the like. Though a copyist, he was also a skillful adapter and a designer of great originality. It was he who practically introduced the exterior columnar porch to Colonial, for almost exceptionless, the buildings of the tide-water are without them. This is more especially true of two story columnar porches with superimposed pediment, so popular since that time with designers of Colonial. The Jeffersonian designs though correct in proportion and possessing dignity, lack the juicy and forceful freshness of tidewater architecture. The buildings around Charlottesville are from half to over a century later in the date of construction than the other Colonial work herein considered, approximating the beginning of the nineteenth century.

It is impossible to speak of Virginia and old Virginia family homes without some expression of regret that they are passing away, for each year sees some of these old land marks destroyed

INTRODUCTION

by fire, and others through unavoidable neglect falling to a sad rack and ruin. It is the more regrettable when is seen the pride that has been stamped indelibly on every house and garden, the mute evidences of the love those families bore to their homes. They have in the past and should continue to furnish to students of Colonial, fresh inspiration for modern work, and remain a never-failing library of information to draw upon.

In so far as this volume will bring before the public and the architect these masterpieces of Colonial and will perpetuate them, we shall feel a sense of satisfaction. And if it shall awaken at all a love for these old grand houses, and shall stimulate at all a demand for correctness of style, so much more will it be a satisfaction and we venture a benefit to a truly American architecture.

STAIR RISER
KENMORE
FREDERICKSBURG, VIRGINIA

NOTES ON MARYLAND HOUSES

STATE HOUSE, ANNAPOLIS
ANNE ARUNDEL COUNTY

Built 1772 from the designs of Joseph Clarke. The wooden dome which dominates the radiating streets of the old town was added after the Revolution in 1784. A fine interior staircase was sacrificed at the time the modern extension was added at the rear.

BRICE HOUSE, ANNAPOLIS

Built 1740 by Thomas Jennings. One of the most dignified houses of Maryland. Roof pitch, 44°. A splendid example of brickwork, main façade composed entirely of headers. Flat window trim. Beautiful carved cornice. Main staircase simple with delicately carved mahogany riser and hand rail. Rooms finished in moulded plaster with carved wood mantels. Now owned by the Carvel Hall Hotel Co. In a fair state of preservation. Plates 1 to 9 and 31.

STATE HOUSE - ANNAPOLIS, MD

PACA HOUSE, ANNAPOLIS

Built 1763 by Governor William Paca. A weak imitation of the Brice House, lacking the beauty of mass and proportion of the original. There are several beautiful mantels in the interior. Now Carvel Hall Hotel.

CARVEL HOUSE, ANNAPOLIS

Built about 1750 by Upton Scott. The main façades of header bricks. Hipped roof of a lower type than most Annapolis houses. Very classic treatment of the interior doorways. Now occupied by the sisterhood of Notre Dame. Much of the charm of the exterior has been destroyed by a coat of paint over the brickwork. Plates 19 and 14.

RIDOUT HOUSE, ANNAPOLIS

Situated on Duke of Gloucester Street. Built about 1763 by John Ridout. The garden elevation contains an interesting triple window which breaks through the main cornice of the house. Main façades of header bricks with the usual projecting course of four bricks at the level of the first story. Plate 19.

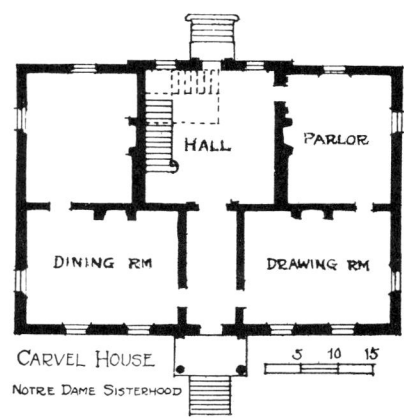

NOTES ON MARYLAND HOUSES

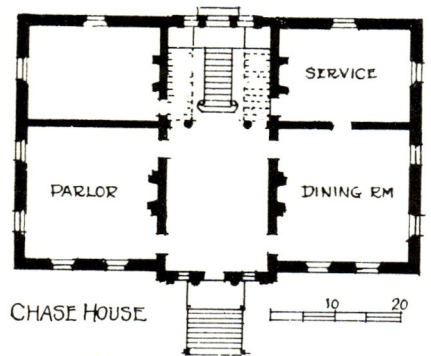

CHASE HOUSE, ANNAPOLIS

Built 1770 by Edward Lloyd. His architect was named Randall. A three story box-like exterior in Flemish bond. Contains a monumental stair hall lighted by a Palladian window on the first landing. The carved interior detail is lavish and beautifully executed. There is a very lovely marble mantel in the parlor, see page 29. Now the Chase Home for Aged. Plates 13 to 18.

HARWOOD HOUSE, ANNAPOLIS

Built 1774 by a Mr. Buckland for William Hammond. A fine example of Colonial city architecture. Bricks laid in Flemish bond. Front and rear doors are of good proportion with beautiful carved detail. Interior inaccessible. Plates 10 to 12.

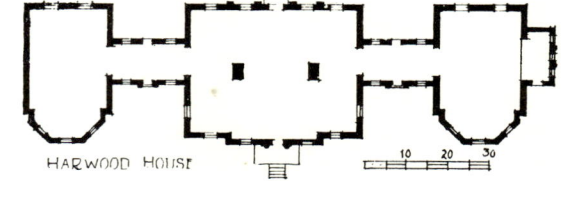

ACTON
ANNE ARUNDEL COUNTY

Built about 1790. The home of the Murray family. Noteworthy for its unusual exterior and attractive entrance porch. The two end bays of the façade are crowned by pediments while the central one is subordinated. The two great chimneys are set their long face parallel to the main façades. The interior rooms are small and the detail uninteresting. The house is in bad repair. Plates 14 and 15.

WHITEHALL
ANNE ARUNDEL COUNTY

Built about 1750 by Governor Horatio Sharp. A refined and delicate exterior of formal plan. Square two story central saloon. The interior doors, windows, and mantels are finished in very beautiful carved wood trim. The stairs are subordinated, being placed in the wings. An open lawn 50' x 400', flanked by gardens, stretches down toward the water. The house has been tastefully restored and is kept in first-class repair. Plates 22 to 27.

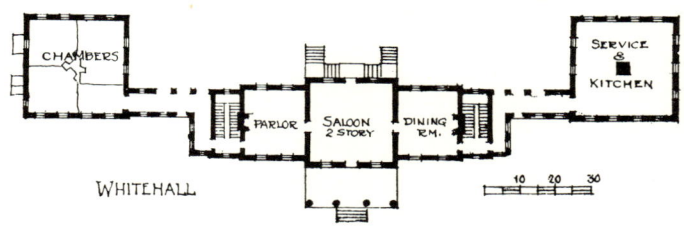

NOTES ON MARYLAND HOUSES

TULIP HILL
WEST RIVER, ANNE ARUNDEL COUNTY

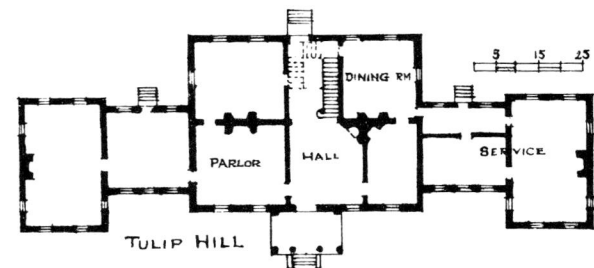

Built about 1750 by Samuel Galloway. On the land front is a one story porch with ornamented pediment. The rear elevation commands a series of formal garden terraces. Over the rear door is a beautifully carved and unusual canopy. Brackets are used in the main cornice on the front of the house but there are none at the rear. The staircase is carved mahogany of very fine proportions. The building is beginning to fall into decay. Plates 27 to 31.

RATCLIFFE MANOR
TALBOT COUNTY

Built by Henry Hollyday. Situated on level ground. The avenue of approach is three-quarters of a mile long. The brickwork is exceedingly fine. The interior wood paneling is well preserved and of good design. The box garden retains its original pattern although now grown to huge proportions. There is still in evidence on the estate the hole from which the clay for the bricks was taken. Plate 32.

WYE HOUSE
TALBOT COUNTY

The original house, built by Edward Lloyd in the seventeenth century, was destroyed by fire. The present wooden structure was erected about 1770. The interior woodwork and hardware bears a resemblance to that of the Chase house in Annapolis. The great pediment of the main house is effective at the end of the long vista, but the lesser pediments of the wings detract from the composition. The grave yard and the brick orangery survive, and the gardens still retain their original beauty.

HOMEWOOD, BALTIMORE

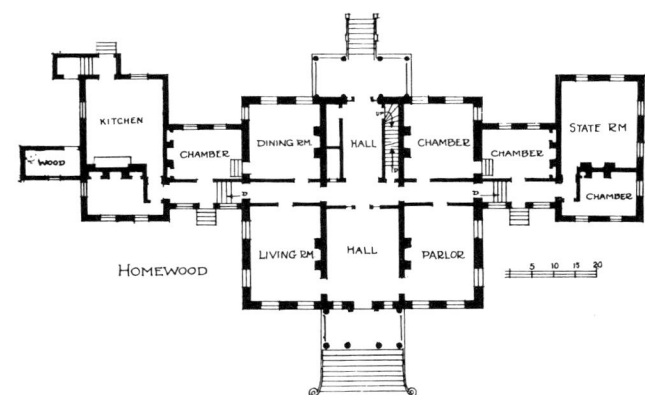

Built in 1809 by Charles Carroll for his son. A small house of very lovely proportions and fine though late detail. It is a representative Maryland house having the two wings attached to the main building by low corridors. Now occupied as the administrative building of the Johns Hopkins University. See No. 16 of Bibliography. Plates 33 and 34.

NOTES ON VIRGINIA HOUSES

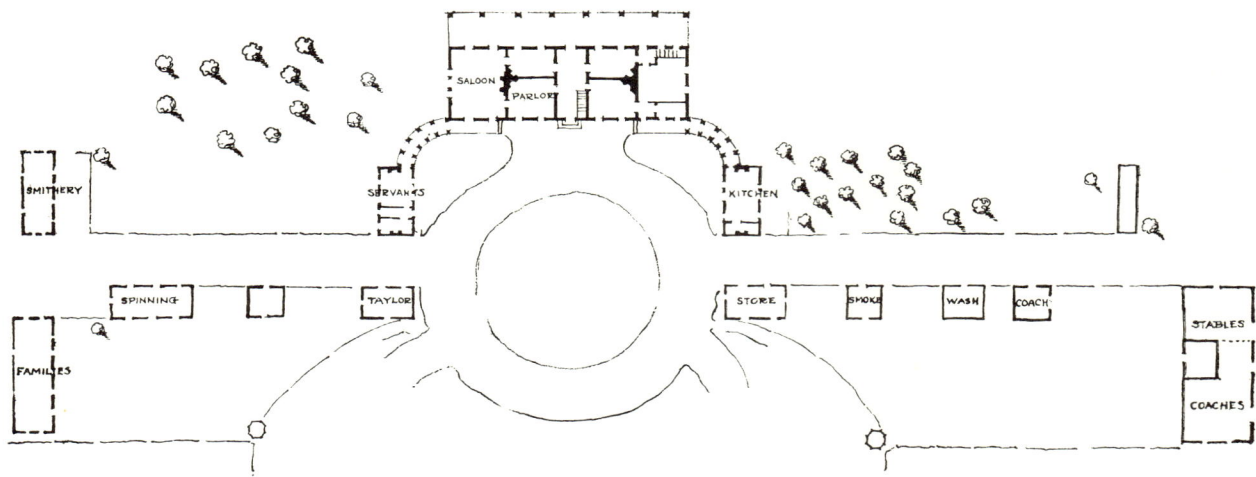

MOUNT VERNON
POTOMAC RIVER, FAIRFAX COUNTY

Built in 1743 and enlarged by Washington himself in 1783 by the addition of two wings with hipped roof, and a two story portico carried across the entire river façade. The north Palladian window was the General's especial pride. The house and out buildings are built of wood. See Appendix A for Washington's letter referring to the enlargements. Plate 97.

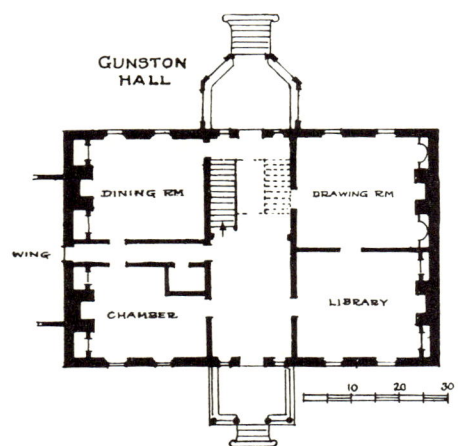

GUNSTON HALL
POTOMAC RIVER, FAIRFAX COUNTY

Built in 1758 by George Mason. The house is small and low and in a setting planned for intimacy and privacy. A long narrow walk bordered by box leads through the gardens and ends at a steep terrace overlooking the Potomac. There are two porticos quite different in spirit, the one on the river side being a Colonial interpretation of the Gothic. The interior is richly paneled in wood and elaborately though somewhat over carved. The house is kept in good condition today. Plates 38 to 40.

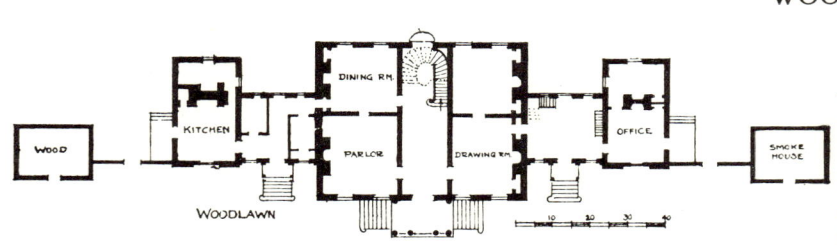

WOODLAWN, POTOMAC RIVER
FAIRFAX COUNTY

Built in 1799 by Lawrence Lewis who married Nellie Custis, Washington's stepdaughter. Dr. William Thornton was the architect. The house has been very much added to and altered. A very simple beautifully proportioned elliptical staircase is the most noteworthy feature. Plates 37 and 38.

NOTES ON VIRGINIA HOUSES

POHICK PARISH CHURCH
FAIRFAX COUNTY

Built in 1769. A square box-like brick church said to have been designed by George Washington. The original interior was lost through being used as a stable during the Civil War. The two doors are of very fine proportion and English Georgian in character. Plates 43 and 44.

CHRIST CHURCH, ALEXANDRIA

Built in 1773. The main body of the church is similar to Pohick, though the presence of the tower gives it a very different appearance. There is an interesting Palladian window behind the altar. The two doorways exemplify a very attractive use of quoins. See Appendix B for copy of original specifications. Plates 41 to 43.

LLOYD HOUSE, ALEXANDRIA

Built in 1796. A fine old house located on Washington Street. The brickwork has not the varied texture of Christ Church or of many of the Maryland houses. There is a simple entrance doorway which may safely be called the best, in a city of fine doorways. Plate 45.

FREDERICKSBURG
SPOTTSYLVANIA COUNTY

The town of Fredericksburg, although the center of a group of famous houses of which Chatham, built 1780, and Brompton are typical, derives its chief charm from the small old houses along the main street. There are many fine doorways, sloping slate roofs with quaint dormers, and massively proportioned chimneys. Plates 46 and 48.

HOUSE IN FREDERICKSBURG

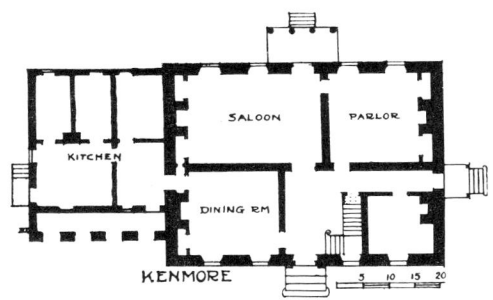

KENMORE, FREDERICKSBURG

Built in 1753 by Colonel Fielding Lewis, who married Betty, eldest sister of George Washington. A house massive in proportion with walls marred by paint. Its chief interest is in the ornamental plaster work of the ceilings and mantels, executed by Hessian prisoners captured at the battle of Trenton. There is a fine mahogany staircase now painted white. The risers are ornamented with an unusual delicately carved ivy leaf. Plates 49 to 52 and page 10.

NOTES ON VIRGINIA HOUSES

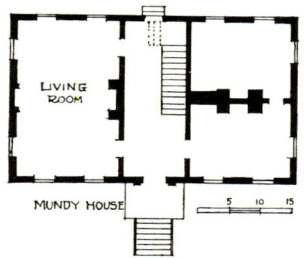

MUNDY HOUSE, DUMFRIES
PRINCE WILLIAM COUNTY

Built in 1756. A small brick house, all headers in the front façade, but with poor exterior detail. It contained until recently a very fine room, done in an unusual manner with a low wainscote and denticulated cornice. Plates 47 and 48.

STRATFORD
POTOMAC RIVER, WESTMORELAND COUNTY

Erected 1731 by Colonel Thomas Lee. A monumental house built on the H plan and dominated by two groups of arched chimneys. The living rooms and the main hall, or saloon as it was called, with high coved ceiling have been placed in the second story and are reached directly by long flights of steps. The house was the birthplace of General Robert E. Lee. Plate 53.

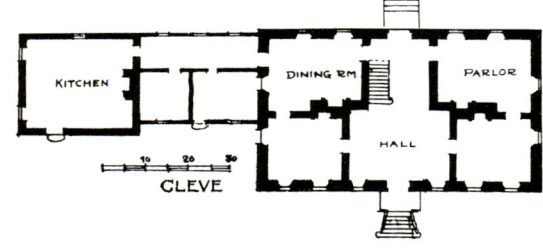

CLEVE
RAPPAHANNOCK RIVER, KING GEORGE COUNTY

Built in 1754 by Charles Carter. Quoins are used in the treatment of the windows, doors, and corners of the building. The interior was gutted by fire in 1800 and restored in crude carpenter's imitation of Colonial mouldings. Plate 54.

GAY MONT
RAPPAHANNOCK RIVER, CAROLINE COUNTY

Built about 1725 by a Mr. Catlett. Stucco wings have been added to the original frame building creating an unusual plan. The house is chiefly noteworty for the old-fashioned picture wall paper which still remains finely preserved in the entrance hall and dining room. Plate 54.

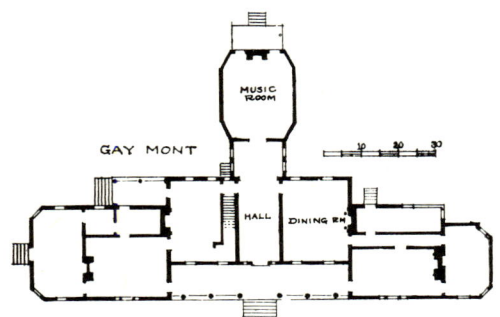

TAPPAHANNOCK
ESSEX COUNTY

The small town of Tappahannock on the Rappahannock River has many charming old houses. The old Brockenborough house has a very lovely vestibule on the river side. Plate 55.

NOTES ON VIRGINIA HOUSES

BLANDFIELD
RAPPAHANNOCK RIVER, ESSEX COUNTY

Built about 1730 by Colonel William Beverley. A large roomy house connected by passages with its wings. On the interior little detail of interest remains. Plate 56

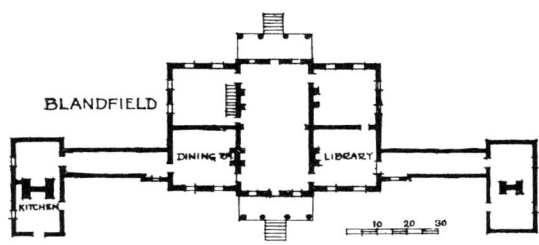

BROOK'S BANK
RAPPAHANNOCK RIVER, ESSEX COUNTY

Built in the latter half of the eighteenth century. A small brick house of fine proportions with dominating chimneys. The delicate interior circular staircase is given an unusual arrangement. Plate 56.

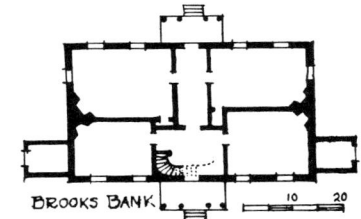

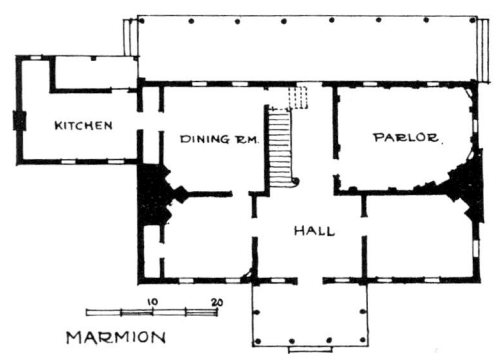

MARMION
KING GEORGE COUNTY

Built late in the seventeenth century. There is a freshness and interest in the interior carved paneling. In 1782 a Hessian prisoner undertook to extra-decorate the parlor panels in oils mixed from native materials. The room has been removed to the Metropolitan Museum in New York City. Corner fireplaces are used throughout and half of one side of the parlor is set at an angle. See No. 4 of Bibliography on page 24.

SABINE HALL
RAPPAHANNOCK RIVER, RICHMOND COUNTY

Built in 1730 by Landon Carter. The house is paneled in the heavy but effective Virginia type of detail. The stairs with beautifully carved risers are placed off the main hall. A fine columnar porch was added to the eastern elevation at a comparatively early date. The bricks have unfortunately been painted. The garden retains its old box border and much of its original charm. Plates 57 to 59, and 31.

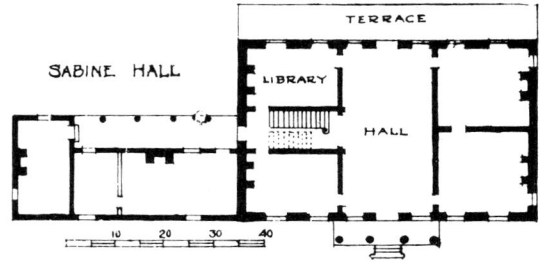

NOTES ON VIRGINIA HOUSES

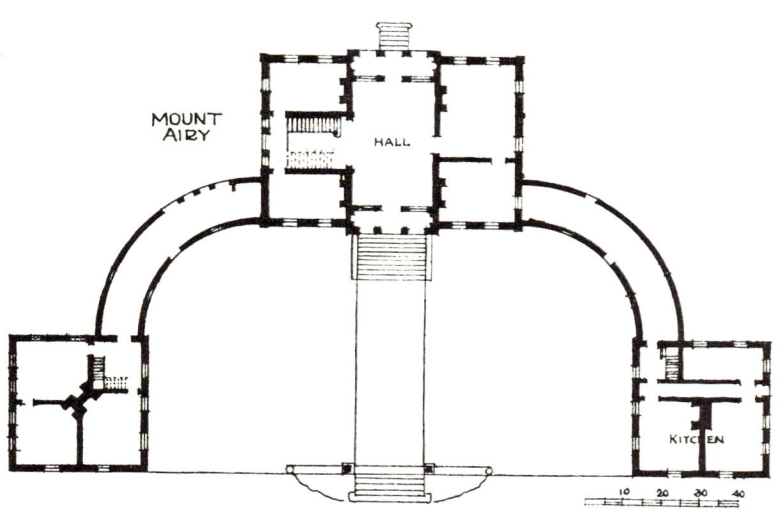

MOUNT AIRY
RAPPAHANNOCK RIVER, RICHMOND COUNTY

Built in 1750 by Colonel John Tayloe. The interior as well as the cornice, chimneys, and roof were destroyed by fire in 1844 and hastily restored with consideration only for comfort and economy. The exterior is of native brown sandstone, with trim of fine white sandstone, said to have been brought from England. The formal setting and character of the house and the monumental scale of the gardens suggest a European designer. A charming entrance motive is supplied by the carved stone urns in the forecourt. Plates 60 to 64.

MENOKIN
RAPPAHANNOCK RIVER, RICHMOND COUNTY

Built about 1765 for Francis Lightfoot Lee, son-in-law of the founder of Mt. Airy. The house is of the same unusual brown sandstone now covered with stucco. Its chief interest lies in its well preserved interior woodwork from which some idea can be reconstructed of the original interior of Mt. Airy. Plate 65.

WILLIAMSBURG
JAMES CITY COUNTY

The majority of the old houses of Williamsburg still contain fine interior paneling and woodwork. The Wythe house on the Palace Green is a noteworthy example. Tazewall Hall, the home of Sir John Randolph and later of Edmund Randolph, though very much altered and moved from its original site, still contains some fine examples of interior Colonial work. Other interesting buildings are the Saunders, Blair, Coleman, Tucker, and Cary houses, Basset Hall and the buildings of William and Mary College. The old Powder Horn on Duke of Gloucester Street was built in 1714 by Governor Spottswood as the powder magazine for the colony. Plates 71 and 72.

NOTES ON VIRGINIA HOUSES

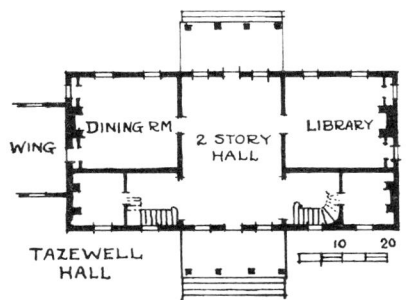

THE COURT HOUSE, WILLIAMSBURG
JAMES CITY COUNTY

Built in 1700 from designs said to have been made by Sir Christopher Wren. A beautifully proportioned small building which has suffered from fire. In the restoration, stuccoed Doric columns, never placed in the original construction, were added to the portico. It is believed, however, that, if it was the intention of the designer to use columns, they should have been in the Ionic order, in keeping with the very beautiful cornice. Plates 69 and 70.

BRUTON PARISH CHURCH, WILLIAMSBURG

Completed in 1715. One of the most beautiful as well as one of the largest churches of Colonial Virginia. Built in the form of a Roman cross. The mass and detail are well proportioned. Of great simplicity, dependent for its charm on the beauty and refinement of the brickwork, which is laid in Flemish bond with glazed headers. The transepts are interestingly composed with arched doorways and round windows above. The interior has a flat plaster ceiling and is most effectively simple in design. Plates 66-69.

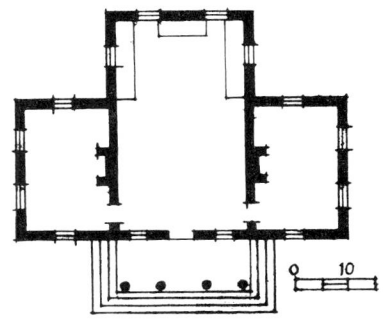

THE COURT HOUSE

YORKTOWN
YORK COUNTY

Yorktown contains some of the most picturesque old houses of Virginia many of which were built with the typical exterior chimneys. The town is dominated by the Nelson house built in about 1740. Although the plan is a formal rectangle great variety has been obtained in the size and arrangement of the interior rooms. The reception room is treated with an unusual application of segmental columns, being about one-third of the diameter of the column at the base. Plates 97 and 98.

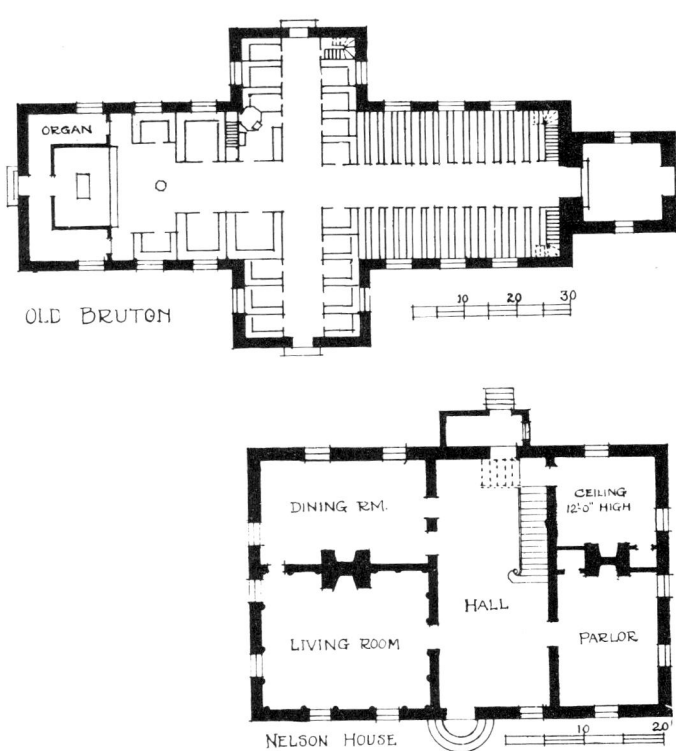

NOTES ON VIRGINIA HOUSES

CARTER'S GROVE
JAMES RIVER, JAMES CITY COUNTY

Built about 1740 by Carter Burwell. The interior is fully paneled with fine detail, which reflects, especially in the great hall arch, the massive character of the exterior. The staircase, which has carved applied newels on the wall side, is especially beautiful. The house is beginning to fall into bad repair. The detached wings are well proportioned examples of cottage architecture.

Plates 73 to 77.

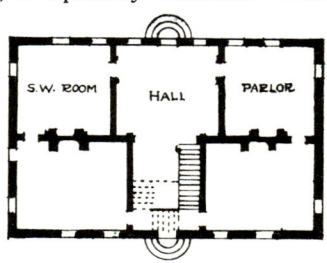
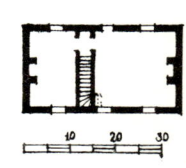

SHIRLEY
JAMES RIVER, CHARLES CITY COUNTY

Commenced in 1660 by Colonel Edward Hill I and enlarged and developed about 1700. A square three story house with pretentious dependent buildings. The two-story porches added in 1800 at front and rear are of unusually fine proportions. The great hall contains a famous "hanging" staircase. The soffits of the steps are boldly undercut. The rooms on the ground floor are all paneled in wood with detail of great purity and refinement. Plates 78 to 90.

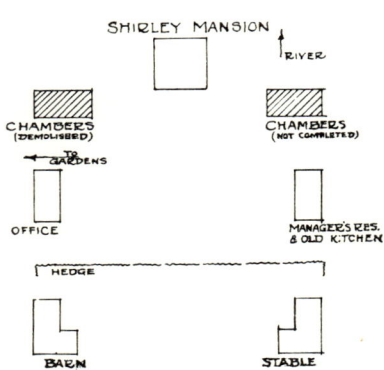

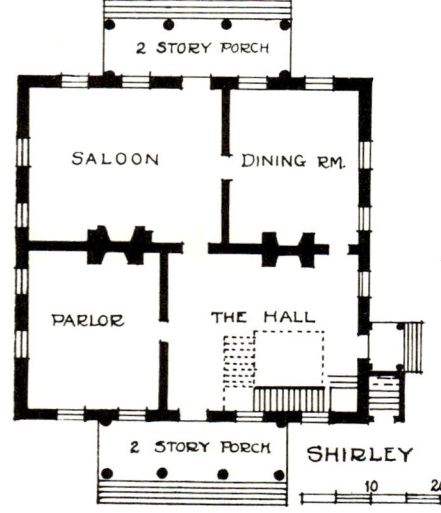

WESTOVER
JAMES RIVER, CHARLES CITY COUNTY

Built about 1730 by William Byrd II. The house has a compelling beauty of mass, obtained by its high pitched roof and tall chimneys, with a very beautiful entrance doorway as the point of interest. The interior detail is elaborate though perhaps not so pure as nearby Shirley. There are beautiful wrought iron entrance gates at the rear and a very lovely fence with ornamented posts. The house has suffered by the rebuilding of the wings and the addition of two story passageways connecting them to the main building. Plates 91 to 93.

NOTES ON VIRGINIA HOUSES

LOWER BRANDON
JAMES RIVER, PRINCE GEORGE COUNTY

Built about 1730 by Nathaniel Harrison II. The sleeping rooms are in the wings which antedate the main body of the house. In the north wing there is a stair with a so-called Chinese rail, a feature common enough in New England but seldom found in Virginia. There is good carved detail in the main living rooms, which has the Virginia characteristic of strength. The wainscoting suffered during the Civil War. The existing porches are unfortunate restorations with jig saw detail. Brandon's greatest charm is in the scale and variety of planting in the gardens. Plates 94 to 96.

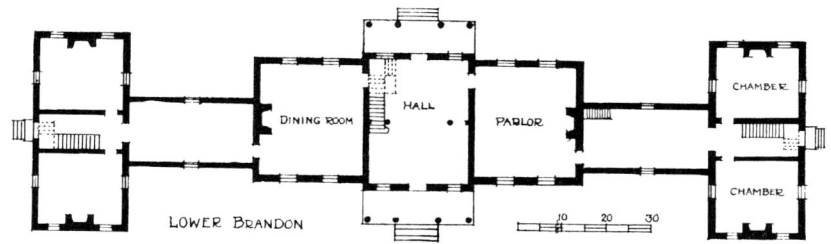

SMITHFIELD AND ST. LUKE'S CHURCH
JAMES RIVER, ISLE OF WIGHT COUNTY

St. Luke's church was built in 1632. Here, as at Jamestown, wall buttresses were used. The windows are round headed with a center brick mullion dividing into two pointed lights.

Smithfield itself is an interesting old commercial town which still retains something of its original character. In the old Morrison house there is a fine spiral staircase confined in a space 7'-3" x 11'-6". It is said to have been built by a travelling Englishman to extricate himself from debt.

BACON'S CASTLE
JAMES RIVER, SURRY COUNTY

Built about 1660 by Arthur Allen. The house earned its title when it was seized and fortified in Bacon's Rebellion in 1676. The unusual triple chimneys and the rough hewn timbers testify to its early date. Little detail of interest survives. Plate 96.

MALVERN HILL
JAMES RIVER, HENRICO COUNTY

Built late in the seventeenth century by Thomas Cocke. A small unusual house of very homelike plan. Great refinement is evident in the brickwork as well as in the carefully studied details of the corner cellar stairs and the arrangement of the chimney nooks. Destroyed by fire in 1905. Plate 72.

NOTES ON VIRGINIA HOUSES

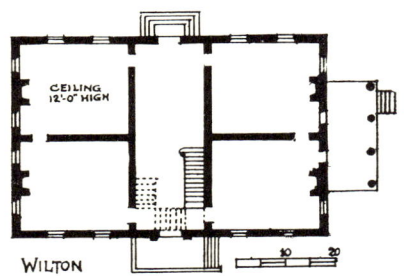

WILTON
JAMES RIVER, HENRICO COUNTY

Built about 1754 by William Randolph III. The chimneys remind one of Westover but the effect is less impressive because of the lower roof. There is a fine entrance doorway. The interior is very beautifully paneled though it has suffered unfortunately at the hands of "restorers." Plates 100 and 101.

RICHMOND
JAMES RIVER, HENRICO COUNTY

It was not until 1779 that the city of Richmond displaced Williamsburg as the capital of Virginia. Its situation was too remote for early development. The town grew to importance in the time of the Classic Revival and is filled with old buildings erected under its influence. Principal of course is the State Capitol, where the hand of Thomas Jefferson was felt. The old Wickam house built in 1812 from the designs of Benjamin Mills contains an especially lovely circular staircase. It is now the Valentine Museum. Veneration for the town of Richmond and the affection which is felt for its old columnar buildings has led to a misapplication of the term "Colonial" to its architecture.

WICKHAM HOUSE, RICHMOND.

TUCKAHOE
JAMES RIVER, GOOCHLAND COUNTY

Built about 1712 by Thomas Randolph. Of unique plan. Contains two very beautiful staircases, the one in the north wing being very elaborately carved. The detail bears a striking resemblance to that of the grand staircase at Rosewell and it is very likely that the same workmen were employed upon it, since the Pages, the proprietors of Rosewell, were related to the Randolphs. Plates 102 to 105.

GOOCHLAND COUNTY COURT HOUSE

A typical Virginia court house with columnar portico. Heavy but not unattractive in mass. Plate 112.

NOTES ON VIRGINIA HOUSES

ROSEWELL
YORK RIVER, GLOUCESTER COUNTY

Built in 1725 by Mann Page I. One of the most pretentious houses of Virginia. There was a great forecourt with semi-circular wooden columnar porticos connecting the wings. The interior was once elaborately paneled. The great grand staircase as well as the rear stair were both richly carved. The house was burned in 1916. Plate 99.

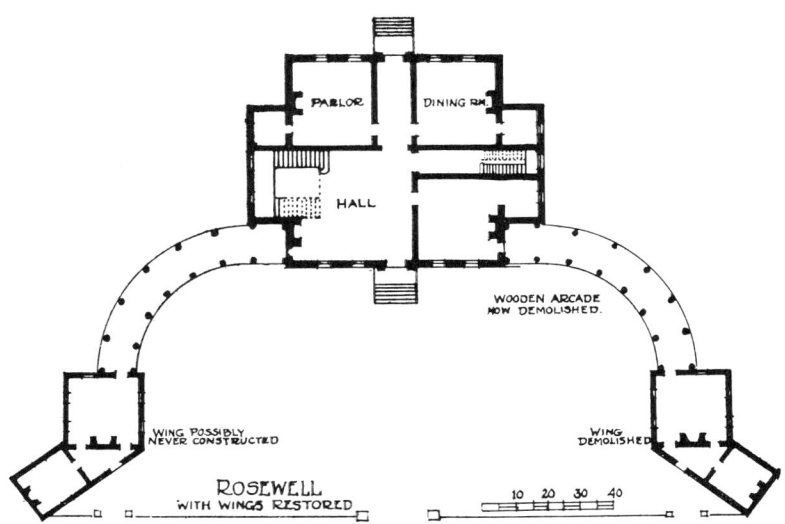

ABINGTON CHURCH
YORK RIVER, GLOUCESTER COUNTY

Part of the building dates from 1660 but the church, as it stands, was constructed in 1765. It is a typical example of the cruciform Virginia church with moulded brick used in the base course and doorway. Plate 100.

MYERS HOUSE, NORFOLK

Built in 1791 by Moses Myers. A typical Norfolk house and a splendid example of the late Colonial city type. The apparent fineness of the ornament and the transition from the carved to the composition detail is to be noted. Plates 106 and 107.

MONTPELIER
ORANGE COUNTY

Built in 1760 by James Madison, the father of the president. In 1809 the house was enlarged under the supervision of the architect Dr. William Thornton. The great portico is of virile proportions. The entasis of the columns begins very near the base. The present owners have greatly enlarged the house and have added another story to the wings. The famous garden is said to have been inspired by the amphitheater of the House of Representatives. Plates 108 to 110 and title page.

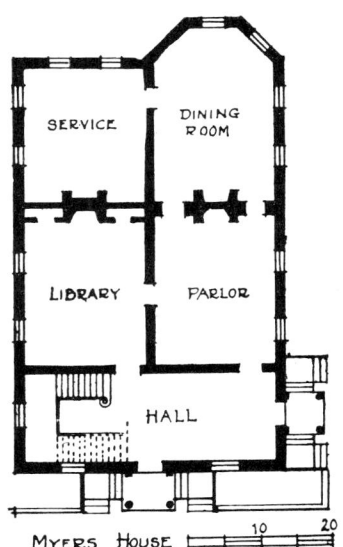

TALLWOOD
ALBERMARLE COUNTY

Built in 1804 by Tucker Coles. The main wing is of brick sheathed with wood. There is an exceptionally beautiful mantel in the living room carved with great freshness of detail. Plate 117.

NOTES ON VIRGINIA HOUSES

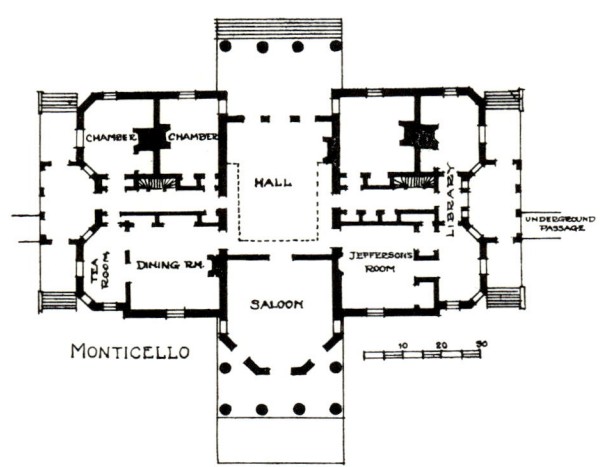

ESTOUTEVILLE
ALBERMARLE COUNTY

Erected in 1830 by John Coles III. Though built in the period of the Classic Revival the house follows Colonial lines. The details, however, are in the inferior manner of the later period. Plate 111.

MONTICELLO
ALBERMARLE COUNTY

Thomas Jefferson's home, commenced by him in 1771 and enlarged in 1796 from his own designs. His work may be called the culmination of the Colonial though in reality it is the beginning of the Classic Revival. Jefferson realizing that American builders were not equipped for their task, directed the way toward scholarly research. Had his followers been one-half as painstaking, the country would have been spared many of the box-like columnar monstrosities, which nowadays are often dubbed "old Colonial." See Nos. 17 and 18 of Bibliography. Plates 114 to 116.

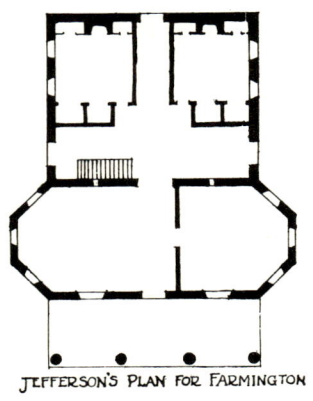

FARMINGTON
ALBERMARLE COUNTY

In 1803, Jefferson assisted his friend George Divers with the enlargement of his house near Charlottesville. Hexagonal terminations as at Monticello were incorporated in the plan. During a temporary absence, it is said that something happened which displeased Jefferson so that he abandoned the project. The capitals are to-day of a size far too small for the columns. Plate 117.

BREMO
JAMES RIVER, FLUVANNA COUNTY

Built about 1814 by General John H. Cocke from plans by Thomas Jefferson. The design has been well executed and its greater simplicity makes it perhaps even more charming than Jefferson's own Monticello. The columns are of moulded brick. The detail is in fine proportion. Plate 118.

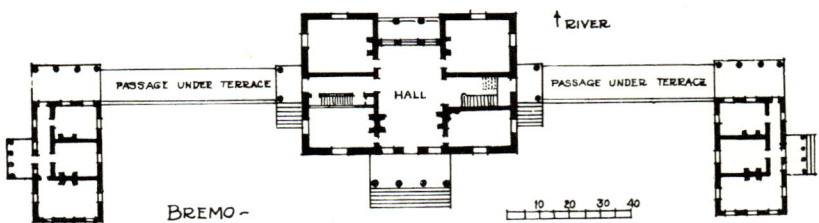

NOTES ON VIRGINIA HOUSES

THE UNIVERSITY OF VIRGINIA
CHARLOTTESVILLE, ALBERMARLE COUNTY

Commenced in 1817. Designed and executed by Thomas Jefferson. One of the few really monumental conceptions in America. Jefferson has worked out his proportion with mathematical accuracy and painstaking devotion to Palladio. The Rotunda or library dominates the head of the lawn. The students' rooms are located in ranges interspersed with professors' houses. Plates 112 and 113.

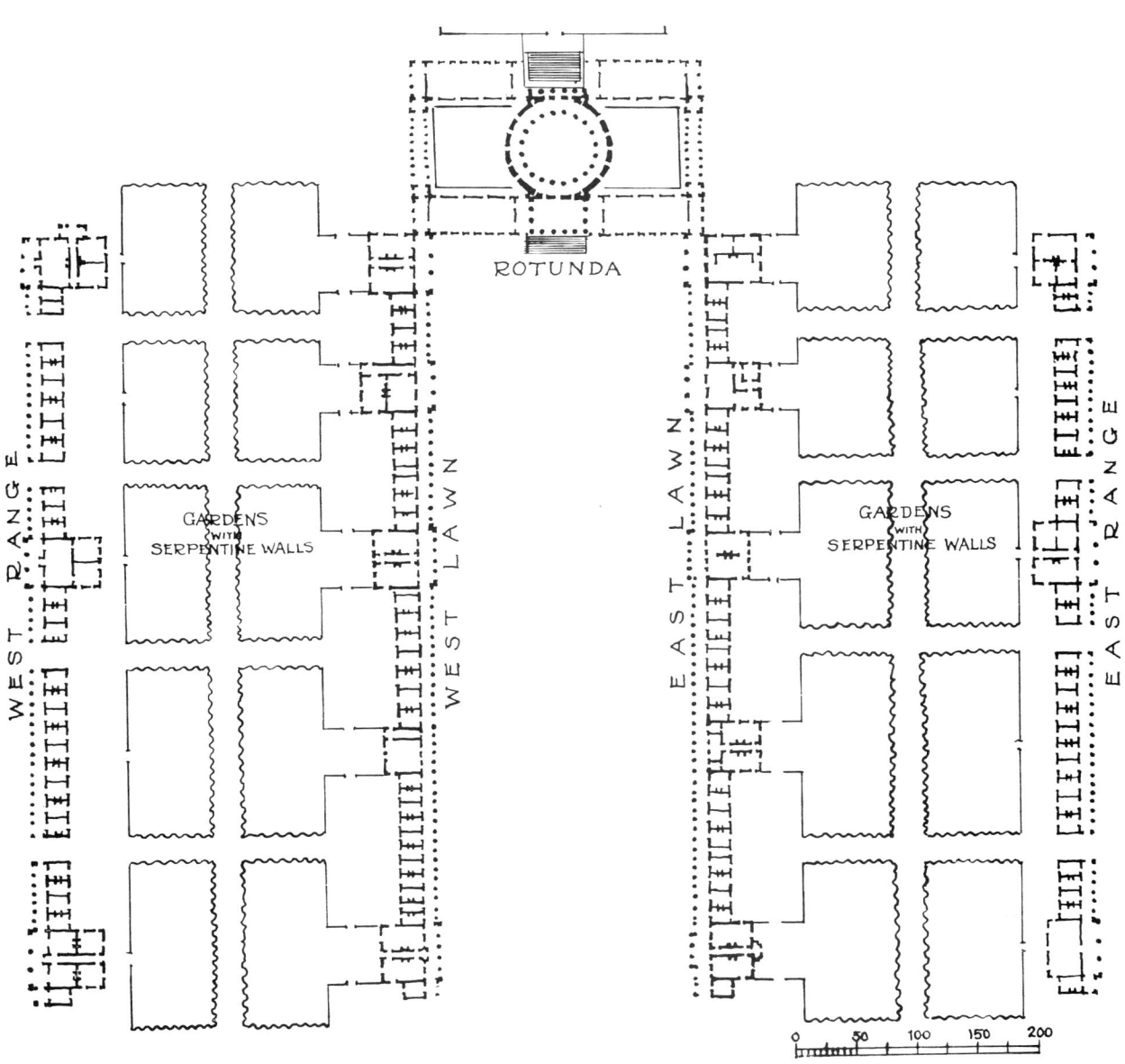

APPENDIX A

Letter from George Washington to Wm. Rumney, 1784

"General Washington presents his compliments to Mr. Rumney—and would esteem it as a particular favor if Mr. Rumney would make the following enquiries as soon as convenient after his arrival in England, and communicate the result of them by the Packet, or any other safe and expeditious conveyance to this country.

"*First.*—The terms upon which the best kind of Whitehaven flagstone—black and white in equal quantities—could be delivered at the port of Alexandria, by the superficial foot—workmanship, freight and every other incidental charge included.

"The stone to be 2½ inches, or thereabouts thick; and exactly a foot square each kind.

"To have a rich-polished face and good joints, so that a neat floor may be made therewith.

"*Second.*—Upon what terms the common Irish marble (black-and-white, if to be had)—same dimensions, could be delivered as above.

"*Third.*—As the General has been informed of a very cheap kind of marble, good in quality, at or in the neighborhood of Ostend, he would thank Mr. Rumney, if it should fall in his way, to institute an inquiry into this also.

"On the Report of Mr. Rumney, the General will take his ultimate determination; for which reason he prays him to be precise and exact. The Piazza or Colonade for which this is wanted as a floor is 92 feet, 8 inches, by 12 feet, 8 inches within the margin or border that surrounds it. Over and above the quantity here mentioned, if the above flags are cheap, he would get as much as would lay floors in the circular colonades, or covered ways at the wings of the house—each of which at the outer curve is 38 feet in length by 7 feet, 2 inches in breadth, within the margin or border as aforesaid.

"The General being in want of a house-joiner and bricklayer who understand their respective trades perfectly, would thank Mr. Rumney for enquiring into the terms upon which such workmen might be engaged for two or three years (the time of service to commence upon the ship's arrival at Alexandria); a shorter term than two years would not answer because, foreigners generally have a seasoning which with other interruptions too frequently wastes the greater part of the first year—more to the advantage of the employer than to the employed. Bed, board and tools to be found by the former, clothing by the latter.

"If two men of the above Trades and of orderly and quiet deportment could be obtained for twenty-five or even thirty pounds sterling, per annum each (estimating the dollar at 4s. 6d.), the General, rather than sustain the loss of time necessary for communication would be obliged to Mr. Rumney for entering in proper obligatory articles of agreement on his behalf with them and sending them by the first vessel bound to this port."

"Mount Vernon, July 5, 1784."

APPENDIX B

Copy of the Specifications for Building Christ Church, Etc.

January 1st, 1767.

"The Church at the falls and Alexandria to be twenty-eight feet from the foundation. That is three bricks and a half to the sleepers, three bricks to the water table, and two and a half from thence,—The Quoins and Arches to be of Rub'd Brick, the Pediments to the doors Rubed work in the Tuscan Order.

The outside of the wall to be done with place Bricks, the Mortor to be two-thirds lime and one sand, the Inside half lime, half sand, the Isles to be laid with tile on Flags, the lower Windows to contain Eighteen lights, each of nine by eleven, the upper windows Twelve lights each, Besides the Compass head the sashes of the lower Windows to hang with weights and pulleys and to be clear of sap—to have a Medillion Cornist under the eaves.

The Roof to have three pair of Principle Rafters, or as the Workmen call it a principal Roof to be framed in the best mannor and to be covered with inch pine or poplar plank laid close to shingle on—the Shingles to be of the best Juniper Cypress three quarters of an Inch thick, eighteen inches long and to show six Inches, the floors to be laid with Inch and a quarter pine plank and to be raised four inches above the Isles the pews to be three feet, six Inches high besides the coping — With doors to all — to be neatly caped with some handsome moulding, the seats to be Twelve or Thirteen inches broad—the out doors to be folding and in Width———— feet—hung with proper hinges—locks and Bars—To be raised pannel on both sides—locust sils to the frames and Architraves on the outside—The Alter piece pulpit and canopy to be compleated in the Ionick Order,—The Walls and ceiling to be well plastered with three coats with a Cove Cornish—the whole to be neatly painted and finished in the best mannor—the Isles to be six feet."

BIBLIOGRAPHY

EARLY WORKS

1. Norman, J. "The Town and Country Builder's Assistant, Absolutely Necessary to be Understood by Builders and Workmen in General." Boston, 1786.

2. Benjamin, Asher,
    "The Country Builder's Assistant," 1805.
    "The American Builder's Companion," 1806.
    "The Rudiments of Architecture," 1814.
    "The Practical House Carpenter," 1832.
    "The Practice of Architecture," 1833.

    The originals were printed in Deerfield, Massachusetts.

    A valuable reprint of the above with plates selected and arranged by Aymar Embury II was published in New York in 1917.

GENERAL WORKS DEALING WITH MARYLAND AND VIRGINIA

3. Adams, Herbert B., "Thomas Jefferson and the University of Virginia." Government Printing Office, Washington, D. C., 1888.
4. Baldwin, Frank C., "Early Architecture of the Rappahannock Valley," Journal of the Am. Institute of Architects, 1915-1916.
5. Bruce, "Economic History of Virginia in the 17th Century."
6. Chandler, J. A. C. and T. B. Thames, "Colonial Virginia," (historical) Richmond, 1907.
7. Chandler, Joseph Everett, "The Colonial Architecture of Maryland, Pennsylvania, and Virginia," (plates) Boston, 1892.
8. Chandler, Joseph Everett, "The Colonial House," (critical) New York, 1916.
9. Conway, "Barons of the Potomac and Rappahannock, New York, the Grolier Club, 1892.
10. Corner, James M. and E. E. Soderholtz "Examples of Domestic Colonial Architecture in Maryland and Virginia," (plates) Boston, 1892.
11. Desmond, Harry W., and Herbert Croly, Stately Homes in America from Colonial Times to the Present Day," New York, 1903.
12. Eberlein, Harold D., "Architecture of Colonial America," (critical) Boston, 1915.
13. Elwell, Newton W., "Architecture, Furniture and Interiors of Maryland and Virginia in the 18th Century," (plates) Boston, 1897.
14. Glenn, Thomas Allen, "Some Colonial Mansions and Those Who Lived in Them," Philadelphia, 1898.
15. Hammond, John M., "Colonial Mansions of Maryland and Delaware," Philadelphia, 1914.
16. Hammond, John M., and Joseph V. Phelan, "Homewood, Baltimore, Md.," Architectural Record for May and June, 1917.
17. Kimball, Fiske, "Thomas Jefferson, Architect," (critical and historical) Boston, 1916.
18. Lambeth, Wm. Alexander, and Warren H. Manning, "Thomas Jefferson as an Architect and as a Designer of Landscapes," Boston, 1913.
19. Lancaster, Robert A. Jr., "Historic Virginia Homes and Churches," (a very complete illustrated historical check list) Philadelphia, 1915.
20. Lockwood, Luke Vincent, "Colonial Furniture in America," 2 vols., enlarged edition, New York, 1913.
21. Northend, Mary H., "Colonial Homes and Their Furnishings," 1912.
22. Polly, G. Henry, "The Architecture, Interiors and Furniture of the American Colonies during the 18th Century," (plates) Boston, 1914.
23. Randall, S. H., "Colonial Annapolis," in the Architectural Record for 1891-1892.

BIBLIOGRAPHY

24. ROWLAND, KATE, "Some Colonial Mansions."
25. SALE, EDITH TUNIS, "Manors of Virginia in Colonial Times," 1909.
26. SODERHOLTZ, E. E., "Colonial Architecture and Furniture," (plates) Boston, 1895.
27. TERHUNE, MRS. M. V., (Marion Harland) "Some Colonial Homesteads and Their Stories," New York, 1897.
28. The Virginia Historical Magazine.
29. WALLIS, FRANK E., "Old Colonial Architecture and Furniture," (plates from drawings) 1887.
30. WARE, WILLIAM R., "The Georgian Period," 3 vols. (critical and historical with plates) Boston, 1900.
31. WORTHINGTON, ADDISON F., "Twelve Old Houses West of Chesapeake Bay," (measured drawings and text) Boston, 1918.

Special acknowledgment must be made to Mr. Robert A. Lancaster, Jr., for permission to use his photographs of Bremo.

MANTEL IN PARLOR
CHASE HOUSE, ANNAPOLIS, MD.

BRICE HOUSE, ANNAPOLIS, MARYLAND

Plate 1

Plate 2

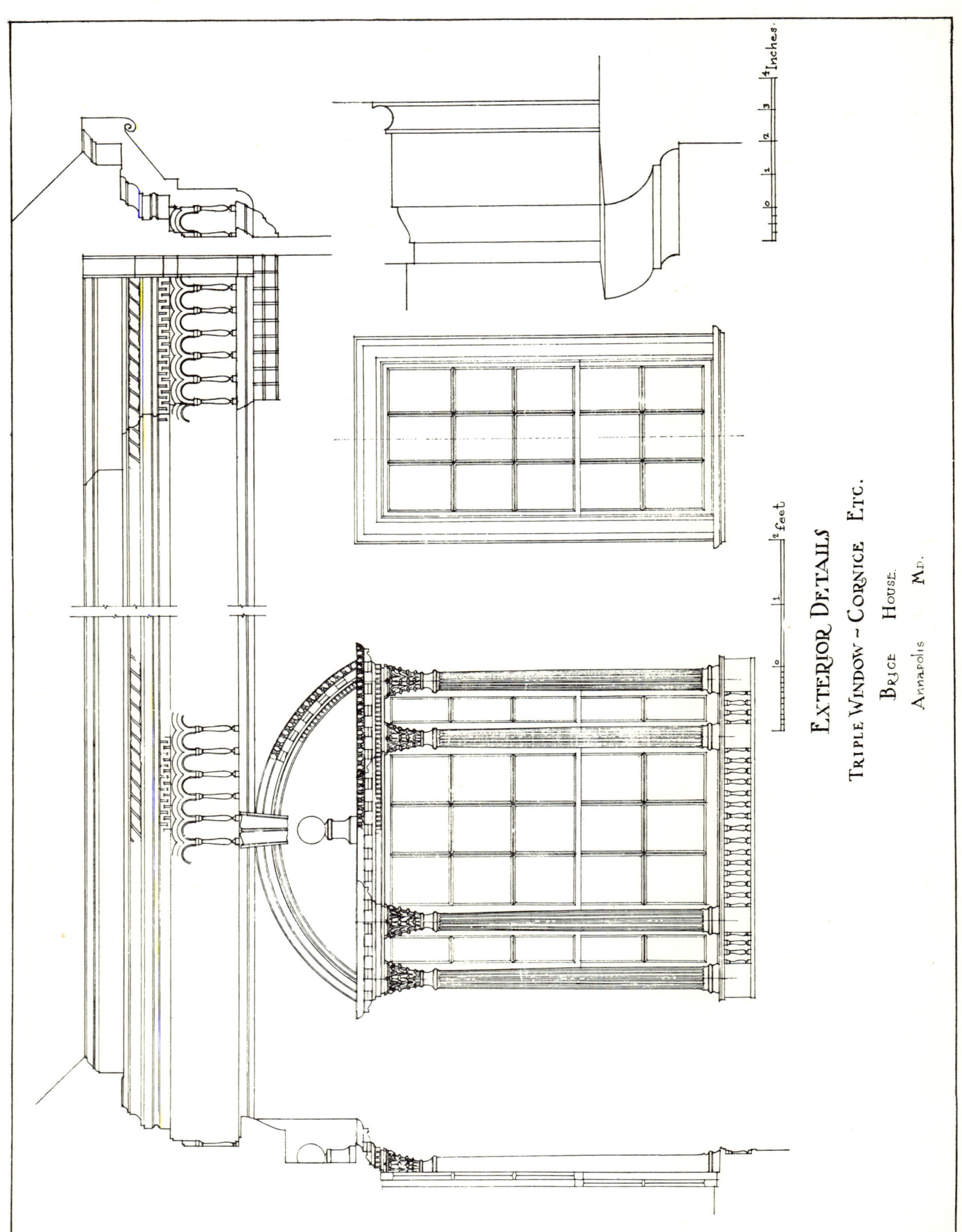

Exterior Details
Triple Window ~ Cornice Etc.
Bryce House.
Annapolis Md.

Plate 4

MANTEL IN LIVING ROOM
BRICE HOUSE, ANNAPOLIS, MARYLAND

Plate 6

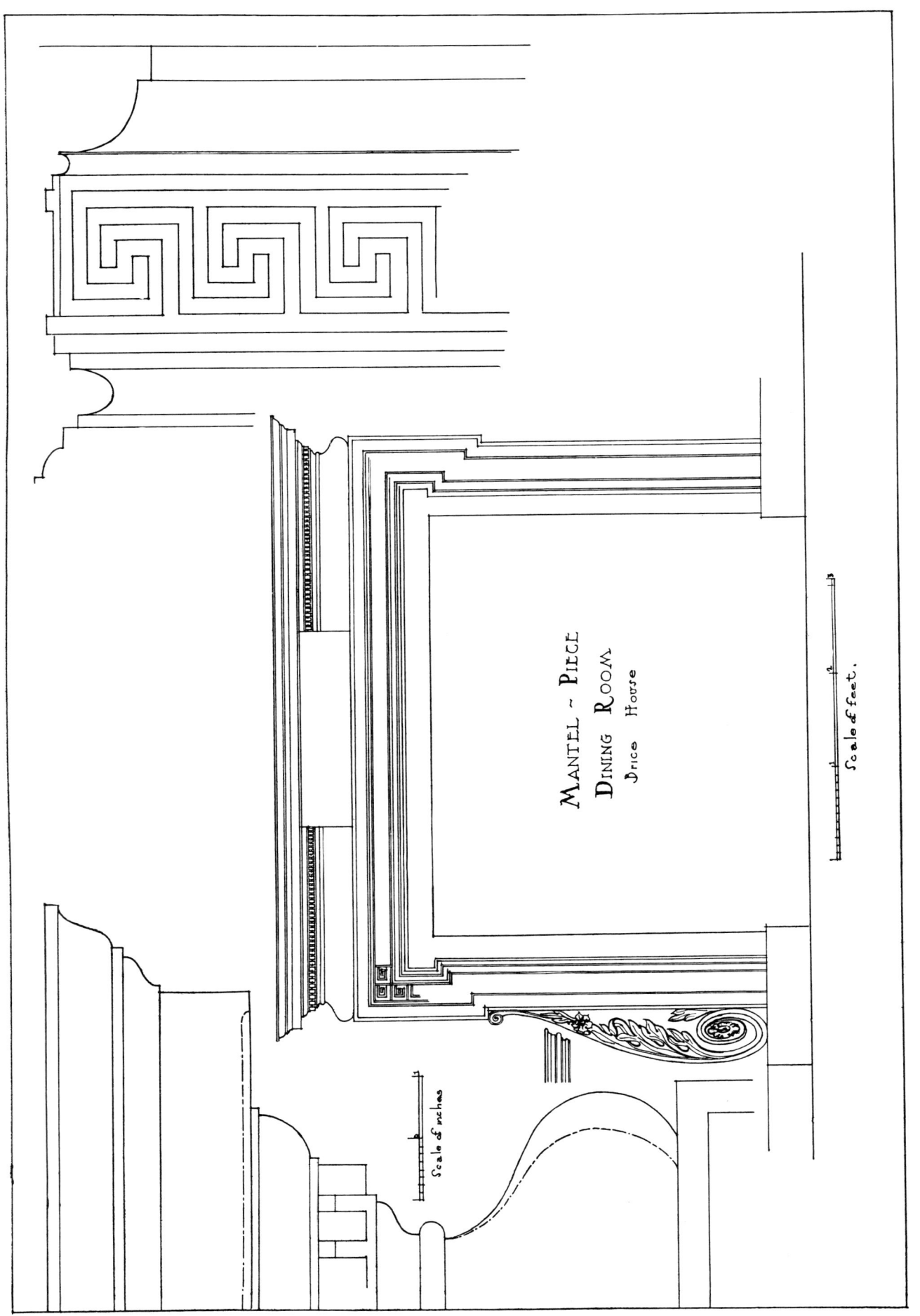

LIVING ROOM

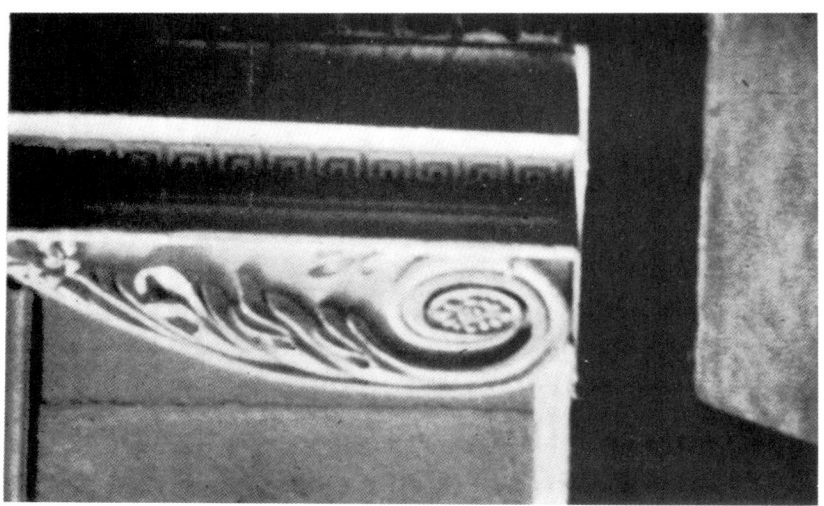

DINING ROOM

CARVED DETAIL, MANTELS, BRICE HOUSE
ANNAPOLIS, MARYLAND

PARLOR

Plate 9

ENTRANCE DOORWAY, HARWOOD HOUSE
ANNAPOLIS, MARYLAND

Plate 10

Doorway
Harwood House
Annapolis Md.

Plate 11

GARDEN ELEVATION
HARWOOD HOUSE, ANNAPOLIS, MARYLAND

Plate 12

ENTRANCE DOORWAY, CHASE HOUSE

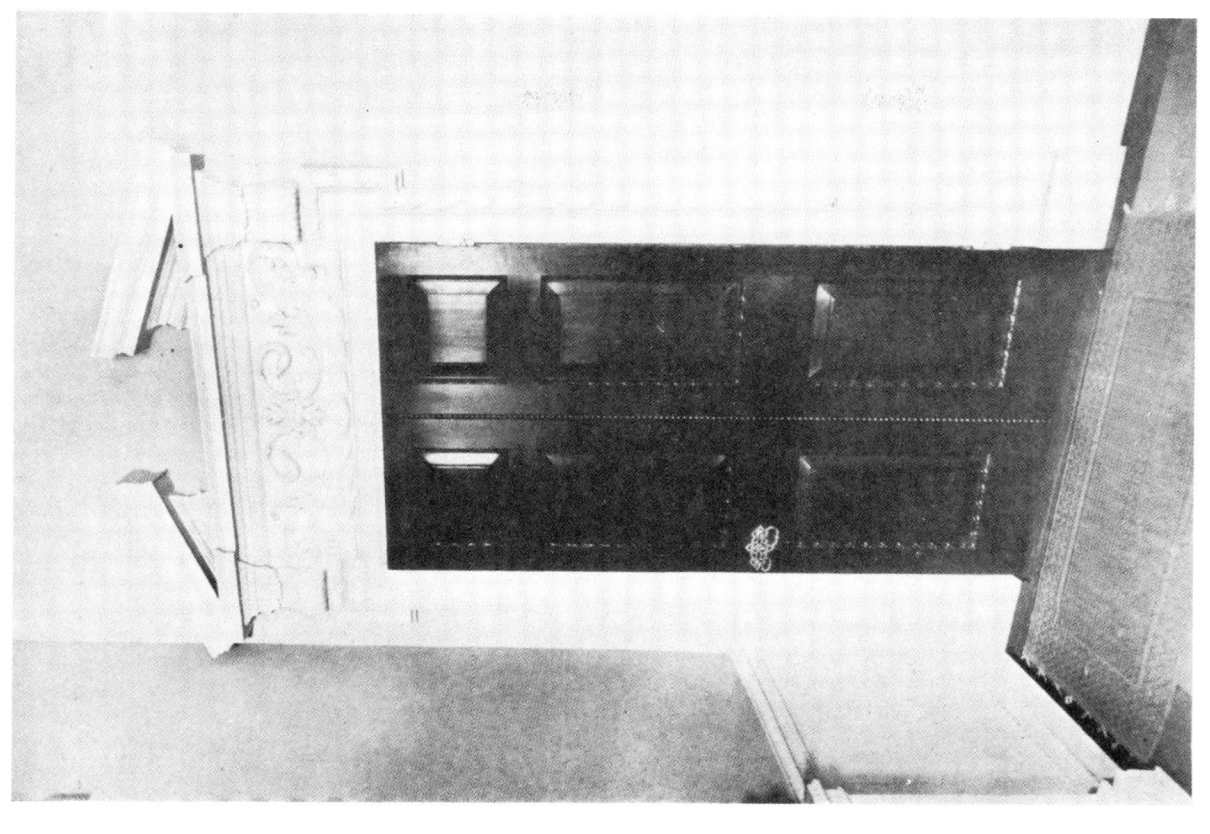

INTERIOR DETAIL, DINING ROOM
CHASE HOUSE, ANNAPOLIS, MARYLAND

REAR, SHOWING STAIR WINDOW
CHASE HOUSE, ANNAPOLIS, MARYLAND

Plate 14

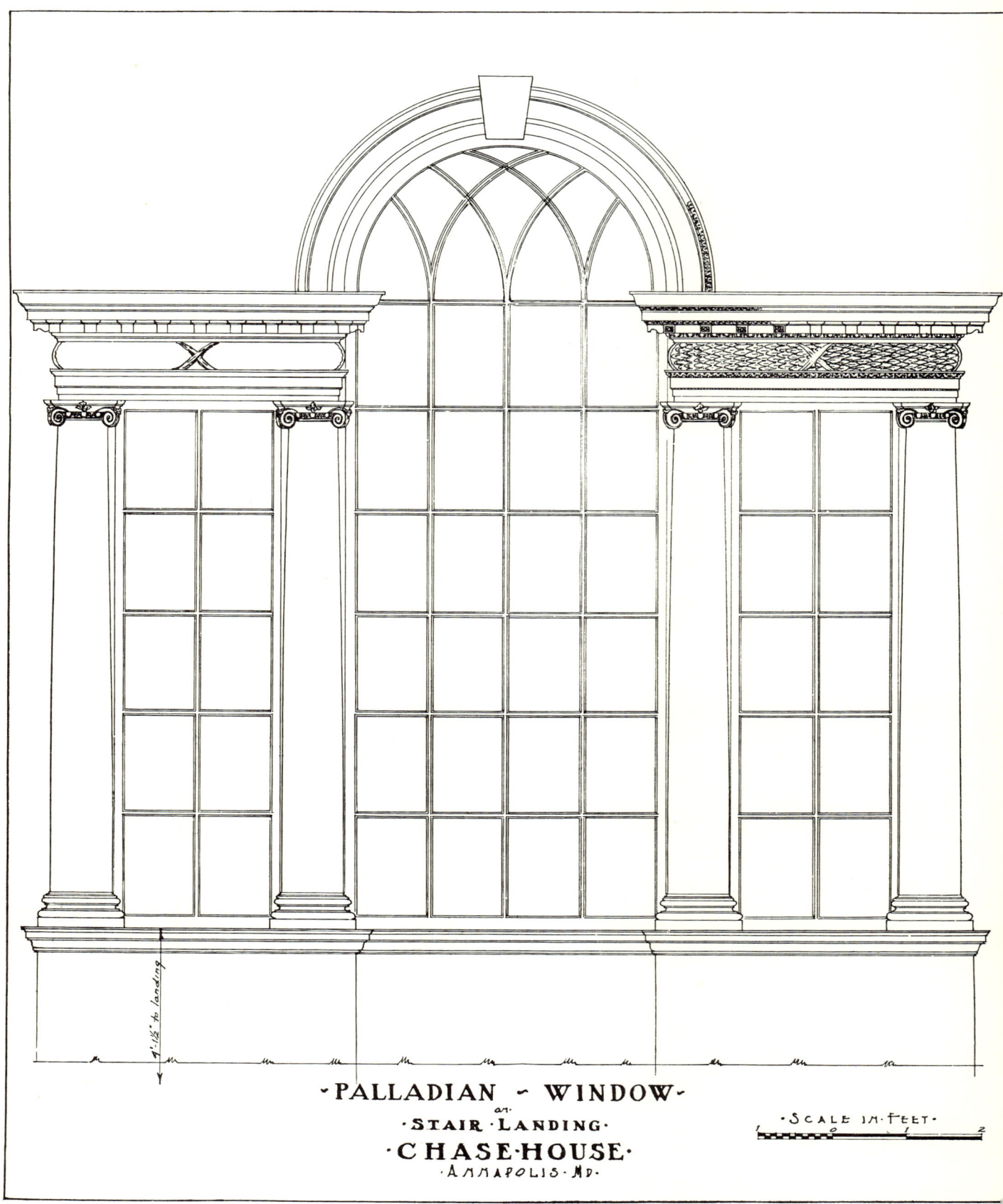

GARDEN ELEVATION, RIDOUT HOUSE
ANNAPOLIS, MARYLAND

Plate 19 GARDEN ELEVATION, CARVEL HOUSE
ANNAPOLIS, MARYLAND

ENTRANCE HALL AND STAIR, CARVEL HOUSE
ANNAPOLIS, MARYLAND

ACTON, ANNAPOLIS
ANNE ARUNDEL COUNTY, MARYLAND

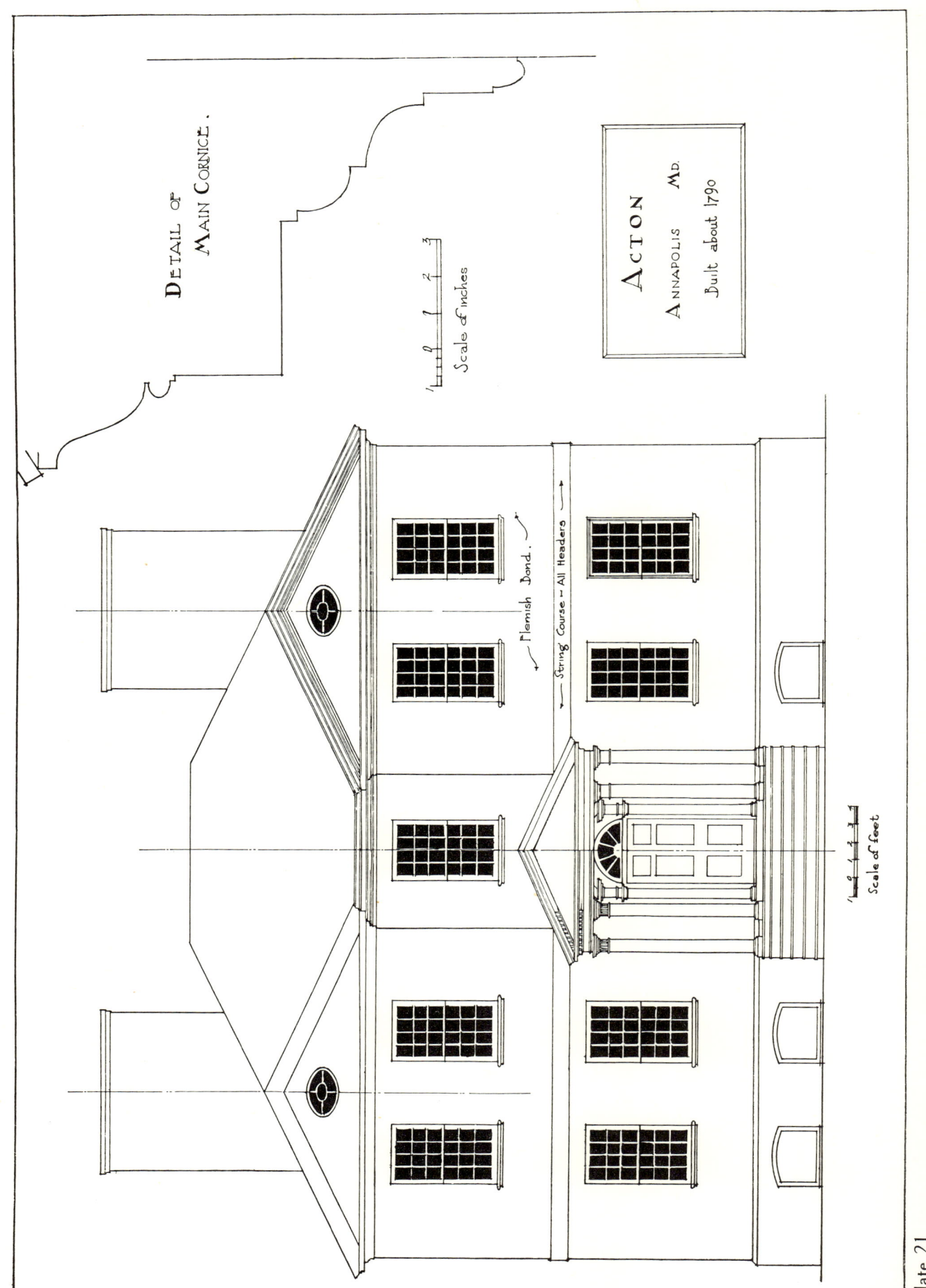

Plate 21

WHITEHALL
ANNE ARUNDEL COUNTY, MARYLAND

Plate 22

WHITEHALL FROM THE OLD GARDEN
ANNE ARUNDEL COUNTY, MARYLAND

Plate 23   DETAIL FROM THE WEST WING, WHITEHALL
ANNE ARUNDEL COUNTY, MARYLAND

REAR VIEW, WHITEHALL
ANNE ARUNDEL COUNTY, MARYLAND

Plate 24

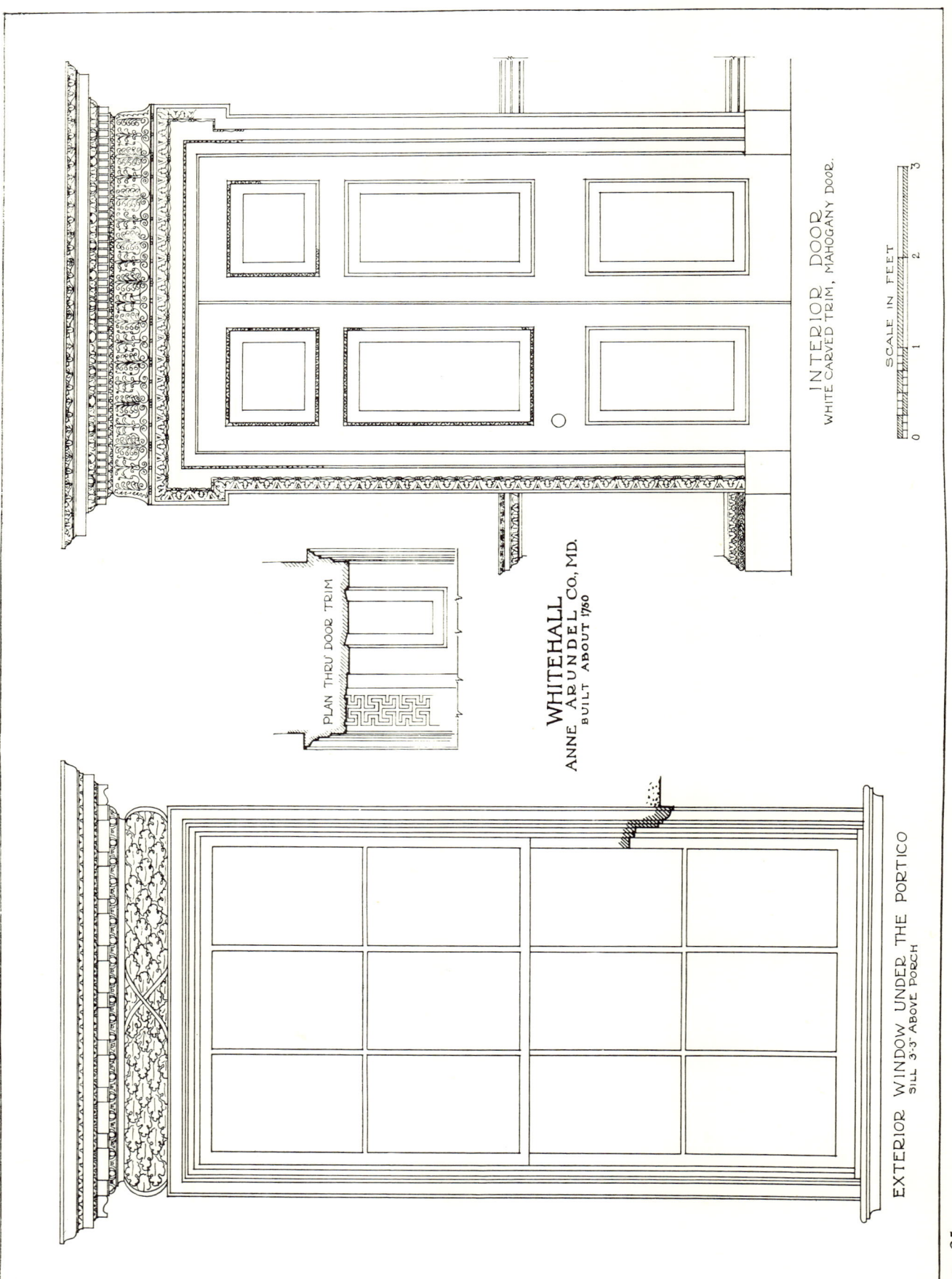

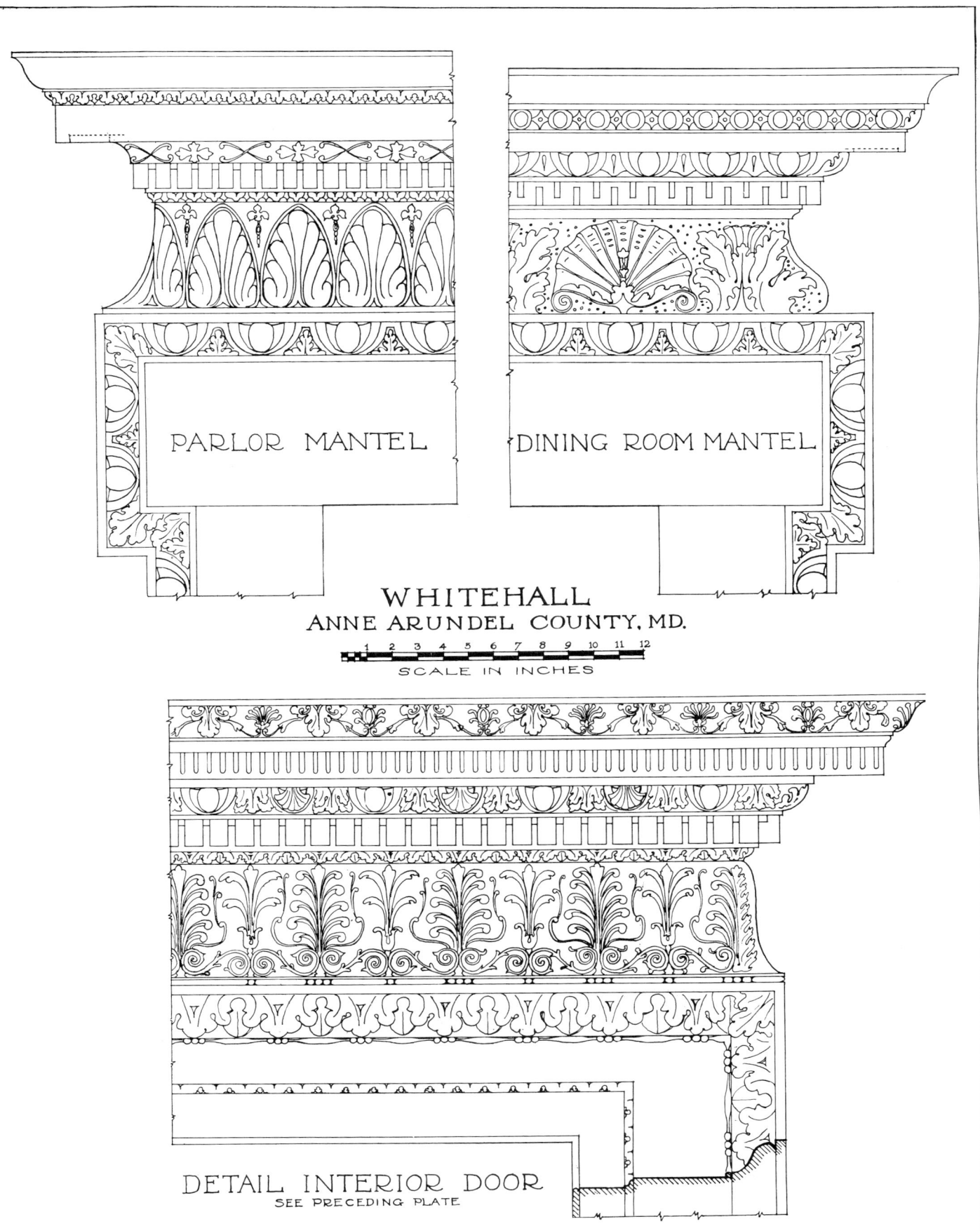

INTERIOR OF SALOON, WHITEHALL
ANNE ARUNDEL COUNTY, MARYLAND

TULIP HILL
WEST RIVER, ANNE ARUNDEL COUNTY, MARYLAND

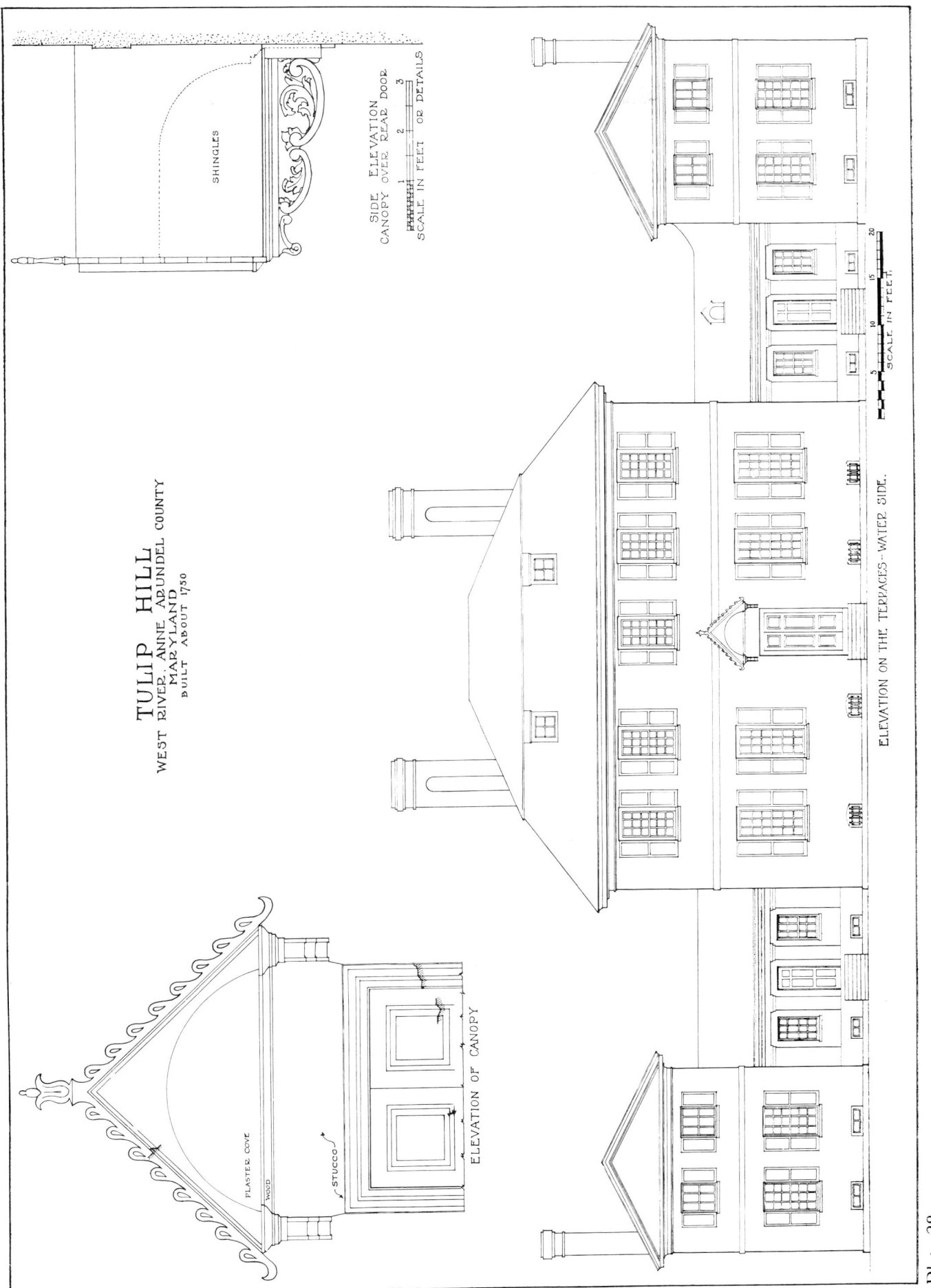

Plate 28

VIEW FROM THE TERRACES, TULIP HILL
ANNE ARUNDEL COUNTY, MARYLAND

Plate 29   THE STAIRCASE, TULIP HILL
ANNE ARUNDEL COUNTY, MARYLAND

ENTRANCE HALL, TULIP HILL
ANNE ARUNDEL COUNTY, MARYLAND

Plate 30

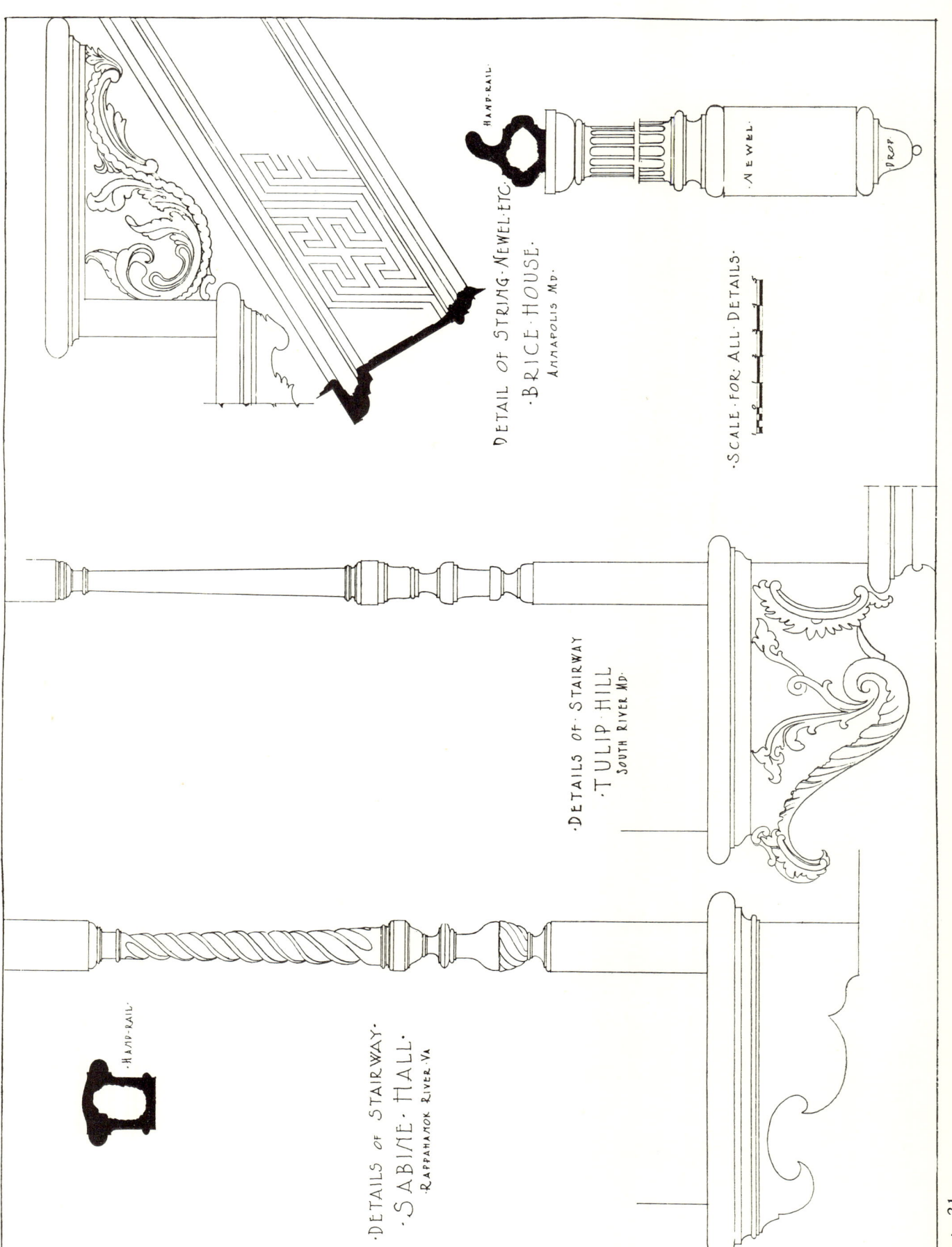

RATCLIFFE MANOR
TALBOT COUNTY, MARYLAND

Plate 32   VIEW FROM THE GARDEN, RATCLIFFE MANOR
TALBOT COUNTY, MARYLAND

HOMEWOOD
BALTIMORE COUNTY, MARYLAND

Plate 33

ENTRANCE PORCH, HOMEWOOD
BALTIMORE COUNTY, MARYLAND

MULBERRY FIELDS
ST. MARY'S COUNTY, MARYLAND

HOUSE IN ST. MARY'S COUNTY, MARYLAND

HOUSE IN ST. MARY'S COUNTY, MARYLAND

FRANCIS SCOTT KEY HOUSE
LEONARDTOWN, ST. MARY'S COUNTY, MARYLAND

INTERIOR, LIVING ROOM, FARMHOUSE
ST. MARY'S COUNTY, MARYLAND

HOUSE IN ST. MARY'S COUNTY, MARYLAND

WOODLAWN, BEFORE REBUILDING
FAIRFAX COUNTY, VIRGINIA

Plate 37   WOODLAWN, THE RIVER SIDE
FAIRFAX COUNTY, VIRGINIA

THE STAIRCASE, WOODLAWN
FAIRFAX COUNTY, VIRGINIA

Plate 38   GUNSTON HALL FROM THE GARDEN
FAIRFAX COUNTY, VIRGINIA

GUNSTON HALL
FAIRFAX COUNTY, VIRGINIA

Plate 39

ENTRANCE HALL AND STAIRS, GUNSTON HALL
FAIRFAX COUNTY, VIRGINIA

Plate 40 THE DRAWING ROOM, GUNSTON HALL
FAIRFAX COUNTY, VIRGINIA

CHRIST CHURCH
ALEXANDRIA, VIRGINIA

Plate 41

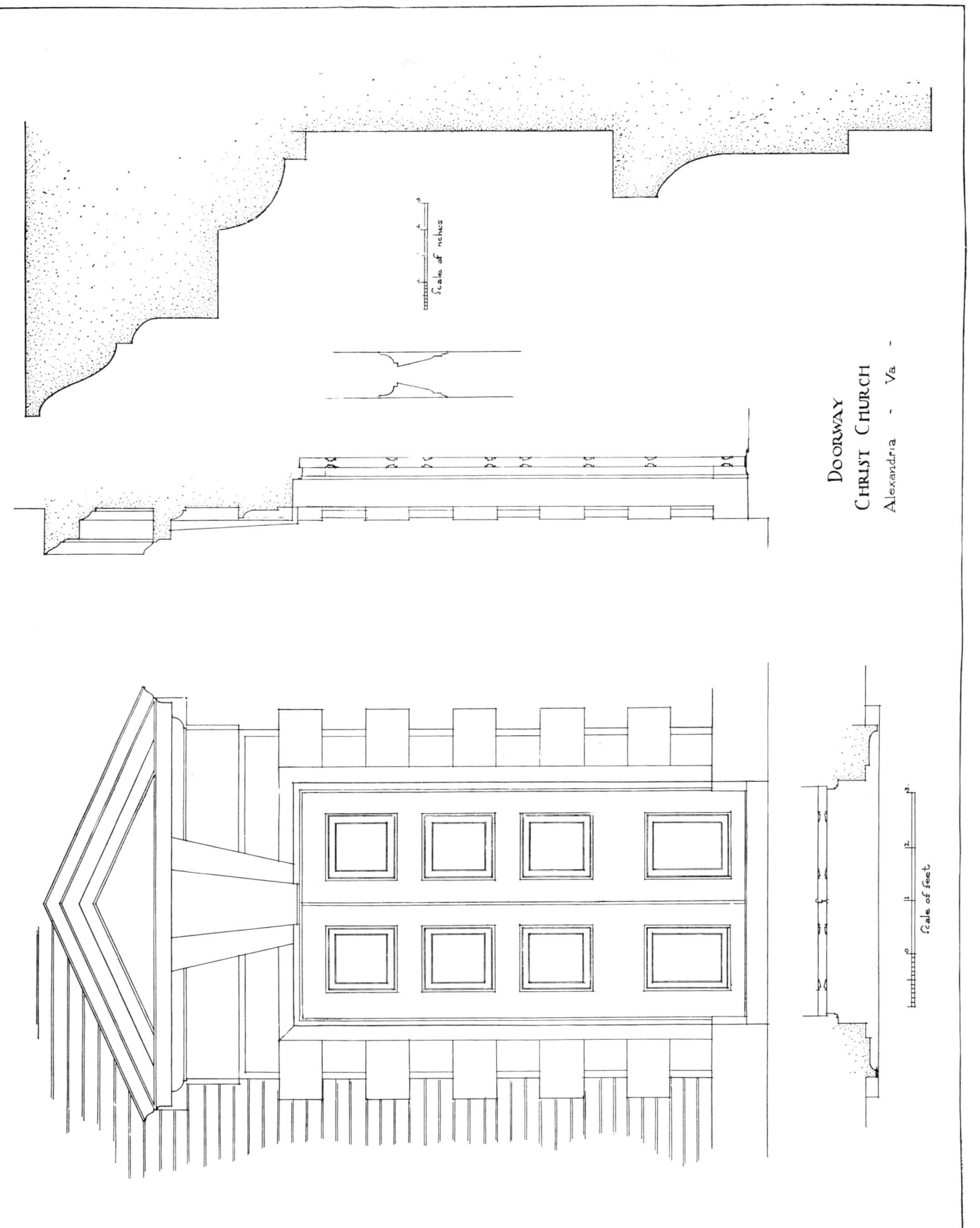

INTERIOR, CHRIST CHURCH
ALEXANDRIA, VIRGINIA

Plate 43

POHICK PARISH CHURCH
FAIRFAX COUNTY, VIRGINIA

DOORWAY, LLOYD HOUSE
ALEXANDRIA, VIRGINIA

Plate 45

DOORWAY, FREDERICKSBURG
SPOTTSYLVANIA COUNTY, VIRGINIA

Plate 46

DOORWAY, FREDERICKSBURG
SPOTTSYLVANIA COUNTY, VIRGINIA

DRAWING ROOM, MUNDY HOUSE
DUMFRIES, PRINCE WILLIAM COUNTY, VIRGINIA

Plate 48

HOUSE ON THE MAIN STREET
FREDERICKSBURG, VIRGINIA

KENMORE
FREDERICKSBURG, SPOTTSYLVANIA COUNTY, VIRGINIA

Plate 49

STAIRCASE, KENMORE
FREDERICKSBURG, VIRGINIA

MANTEL IN PARLOR, KENMORE
FREDERICKSBURG, VIRGINIA

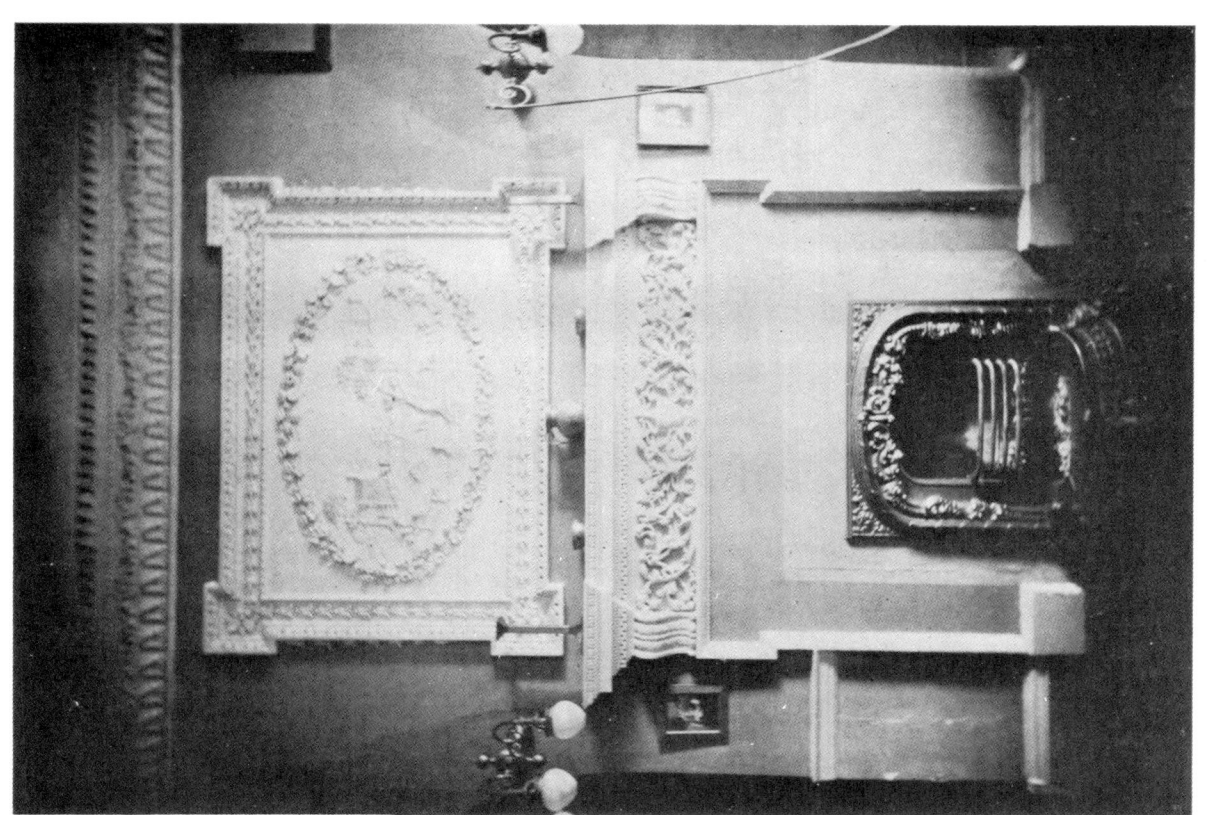

MANTEL IN SALOON, KENMORE
FREDERICKSBURG, VIRGINIA

Plate 50

Plate 51   CEILING IN THE PARLOR, KENMORE
FREDERICKSBURG, VIRGINIA

CEILING IN THE SALOON, KENMORE
FREDERICKSBURG, VIRGINIA

Plate 52   CEILING IN THE DINING ROOM, KENMORE
FREDERICKSBURG, VIRGINIA

STRATFORD, 1730
WESTMORELAND COUNTY, VIRGINIA

Plate 53

CLEVE MANOR, 1729
KING GEORGE COUNTY, VIRGINIA

Plate 54

GAY MONT
CAROLINE COUNTY, VIRGINIA

BROCKENBOROUGH HOUSE

Plate 55

BLANDFIELD
ESSEX COUNTY, VIRGINIA

Plate 56

BROOK'S BANK
ESSEX COUNTY, VIRGINIA

SABINE HALL, 1730
RICHMOND COUNTY, VIRGINIA

Plate 57

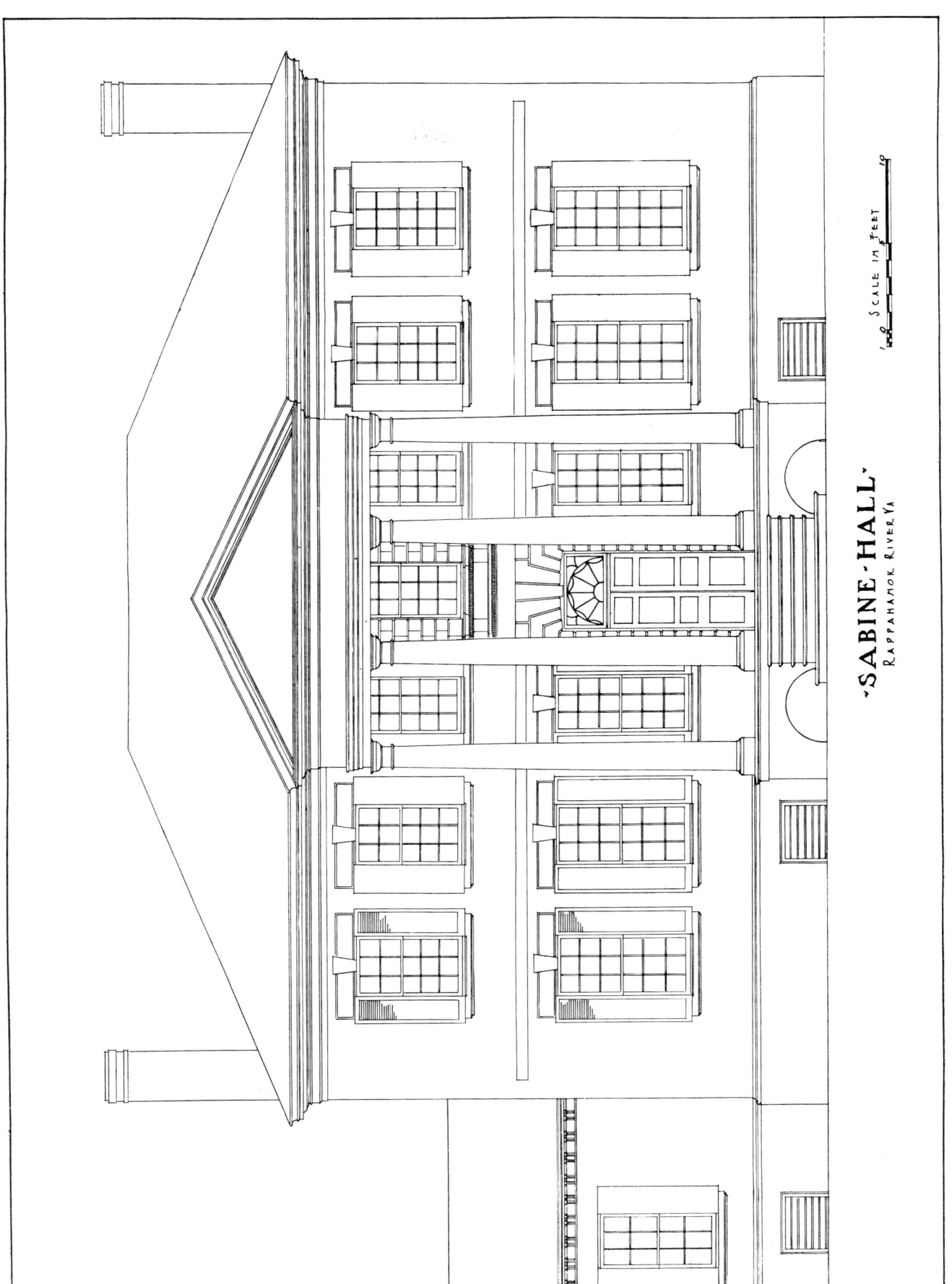

STAIRWAY FROM THE MAIN HALL, SABINE HALL
RICHMOND COUNTY, VIRGINIA

Plate 59

MOUNT AIRY, EAST FRONT
RICHMOND COUNTY, VIRGINIA

Plate 60

MOUNT AIRY, RIVER FRONT
RICHMOND COUNTY, VIRGINIA

Plate 61

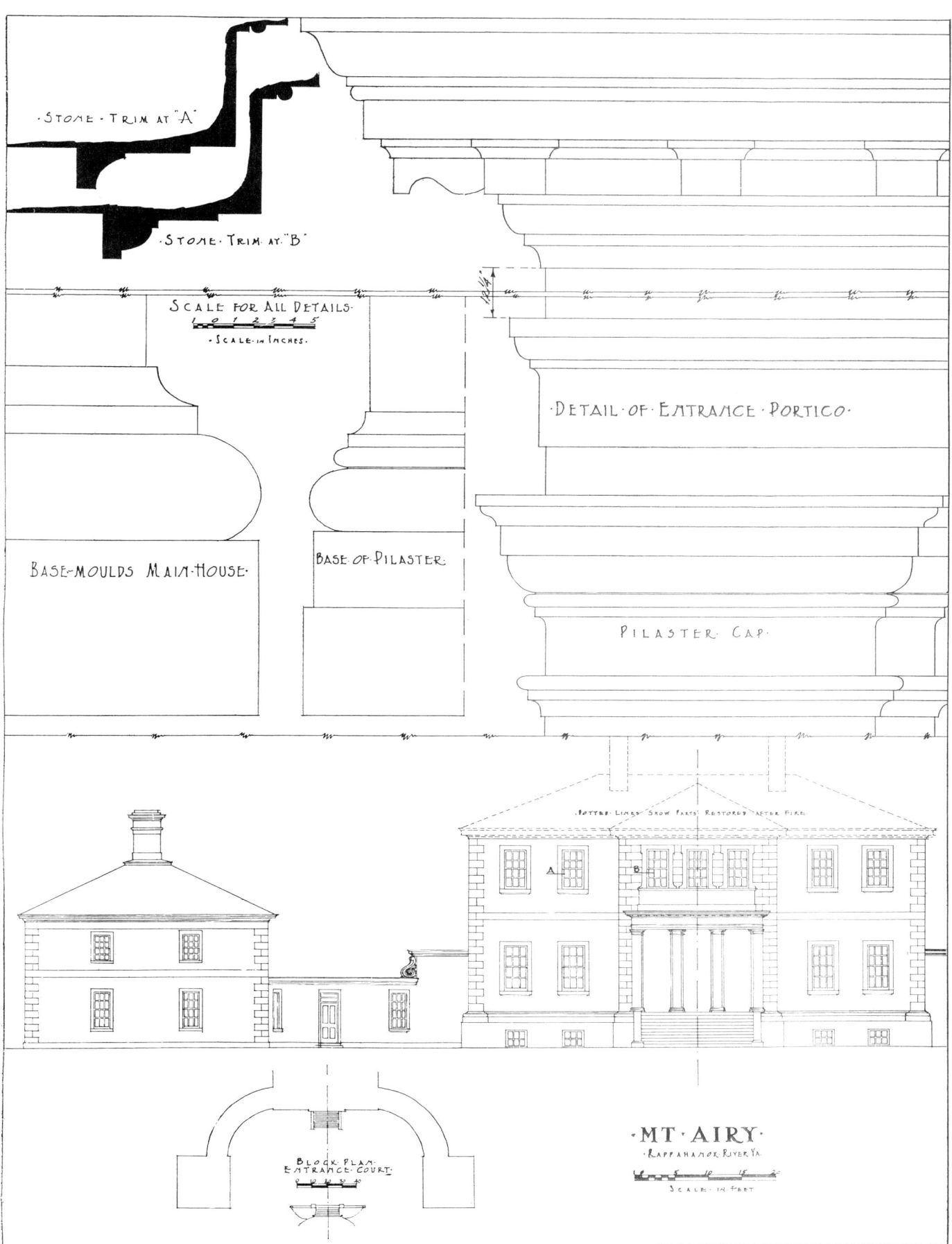

DETAIL, SOUTH WINDOW, MT. AIRY
RICHMOND COUNTY, VIRGINIA

CARVED URNS IN FORECOURT, MT. AIRY
RICHMOND COUNTY, VIRGINIA

Plate 63

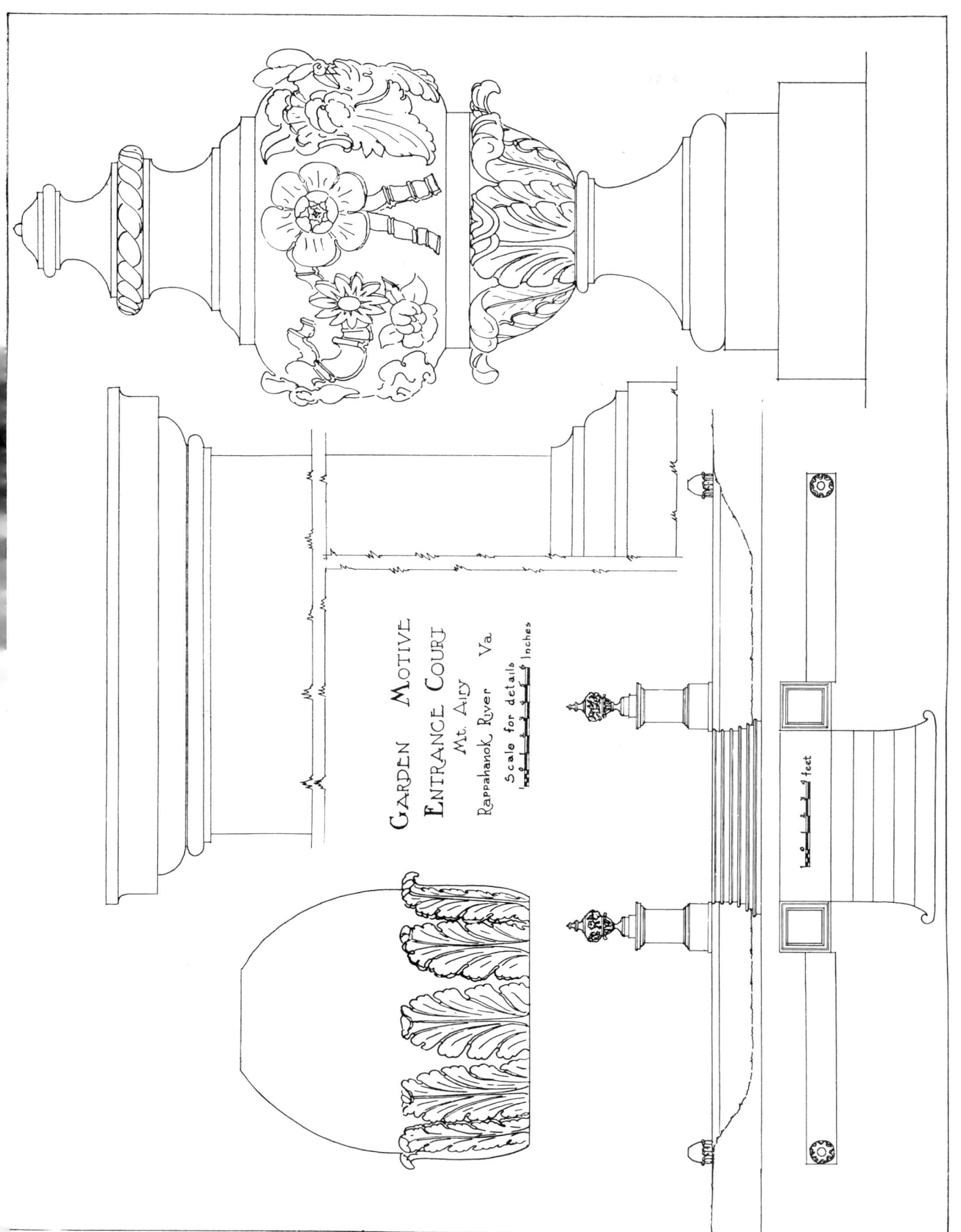

STAIR HALL, MENOKIN
RICHMOND COUNTY, VIRGINIA

LIVING ROOM, MENOKIN
RICHMOND COUNTY, VIRGINIA

Plate 65

BRUTON PARISH CHURCH
WILLIAMSBURG, JAMES CITY COUNTY, VIRGINIA

Plate 66

Plate 67   TRANSEPT DOOR, BRUTON PARISH CHURCH
WILLIAMSBURG, VIRGINIA

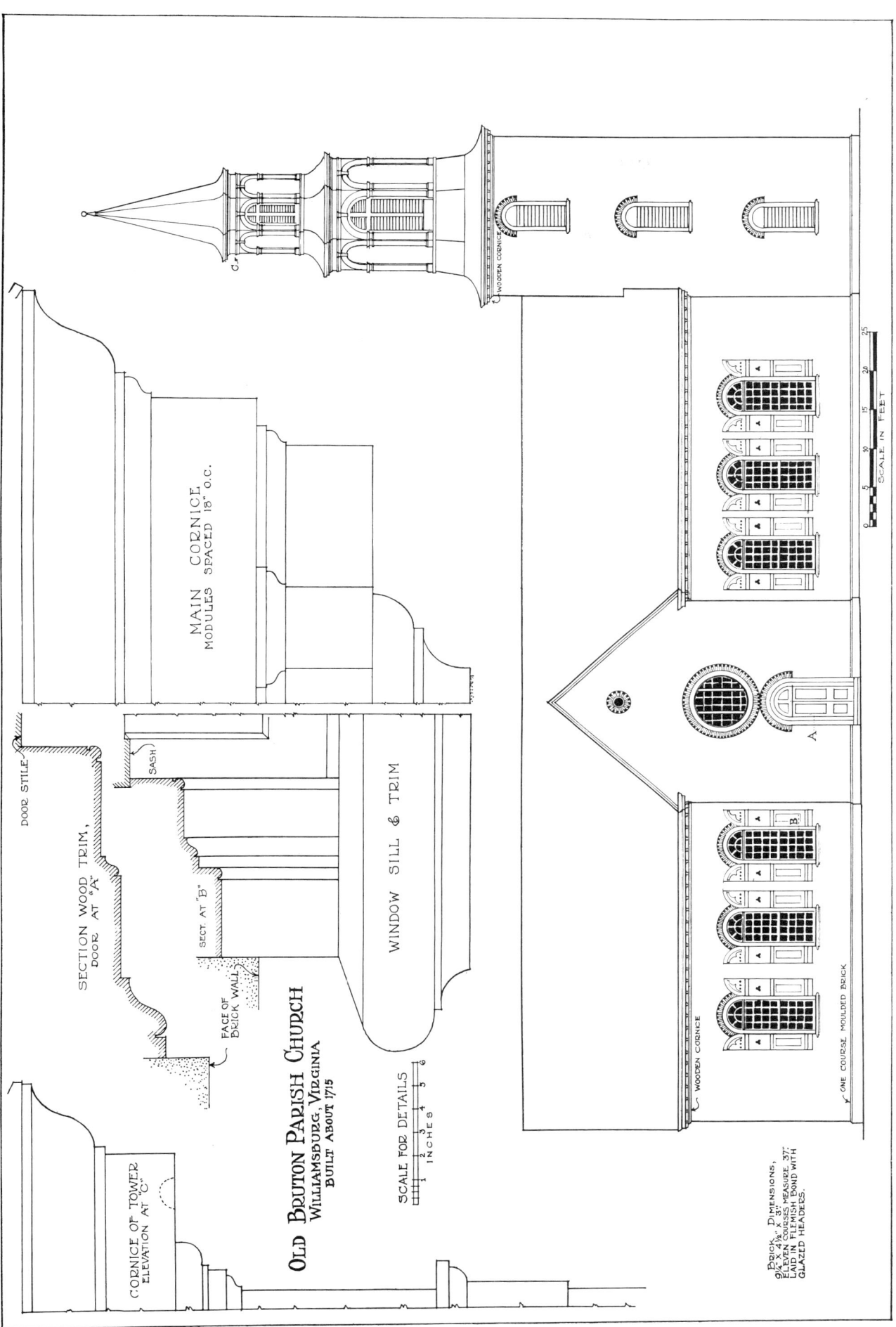

BRUTON PARISH CHURCH
WILLIAMSBURG, JAMES CITY COUNTY, VIRGINIA

THE COURT HOUSE
WILLIAMSBURG, JAMES CITY COUNTY, VIRGINIA

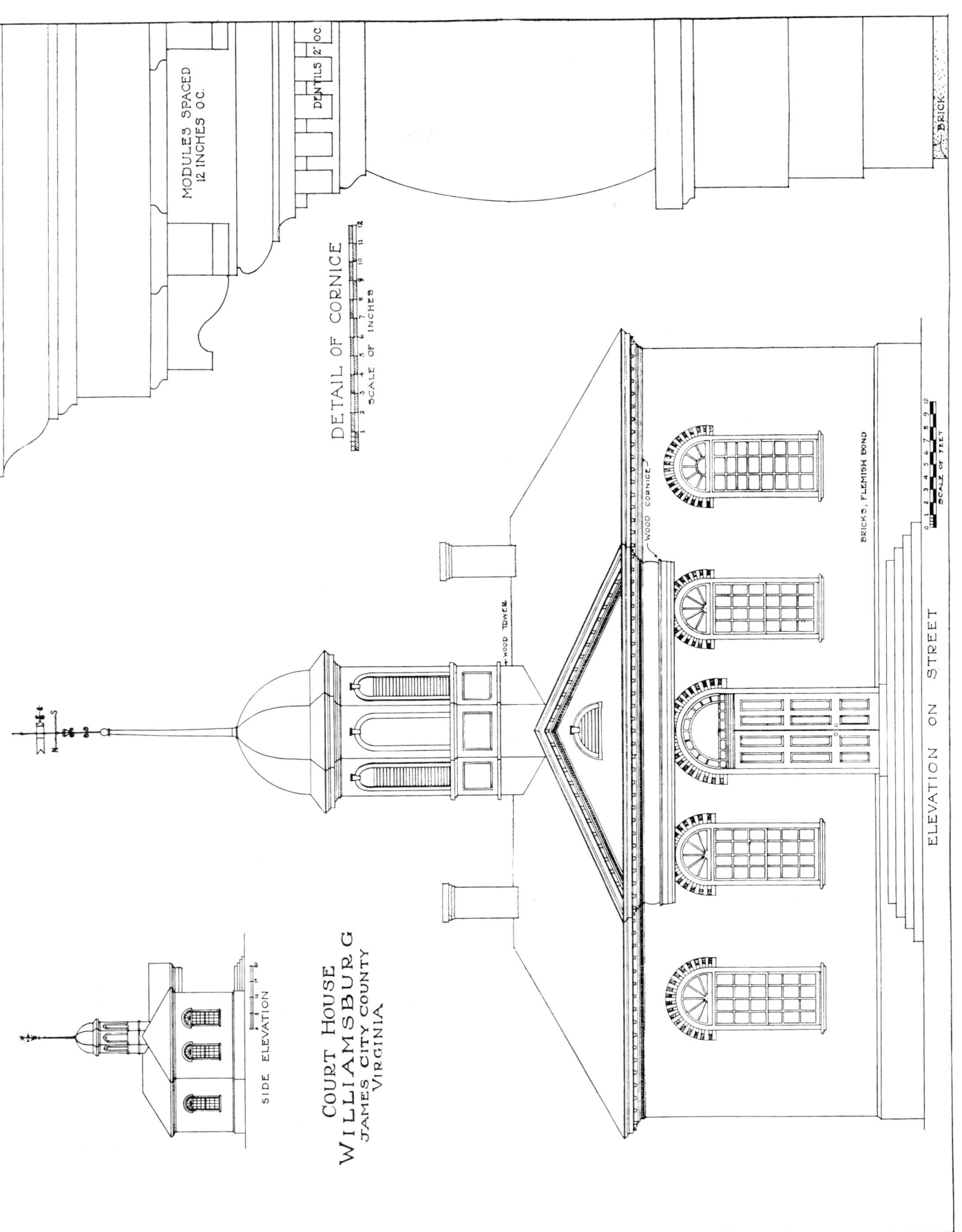

WYTHE HOUSE
WILLIAMSBURG, JAMES CITY COUNTY, VIRGINIA

Plate 71

SAUNDERS HOUSE
WILLIAMSBURG, JAMES CITY COUNTY, VIRGINIA

BASSET HALL
WILLIAMSBURG, JAMES CITY COUNTY, VIRGINIA

Plate 72

MALVERN HILL, (DESTROYED)
HENRICO COUNTY, VIRGINIA

EAST FRONT, CARTER'S GROVE
JAMES CITY COUNTY, VIRGINIA

Plate 73

ENTRANCE HALL, CARTER'S GROVE
JAMES CITY COUNTY, VIRGINIA

Plate 74

Plate 75 STAIR DETAIL, CARTER'S GROVE
JAMES CITY COUNTY, VIRGINIA

DOORWAY TO PARLOR, CARTER'S GROVE
JAMES CITY COUNTY, VIRGINIA

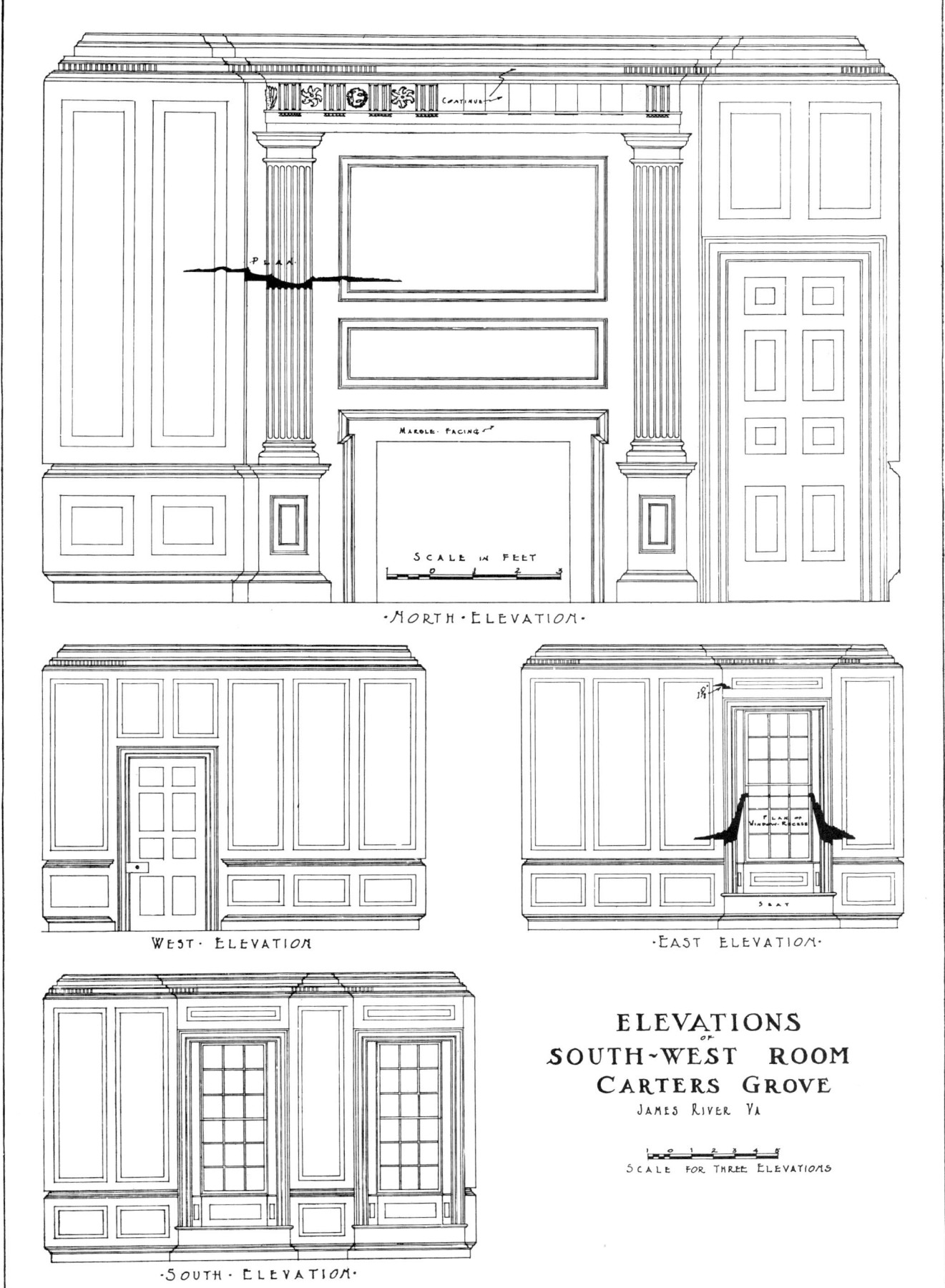

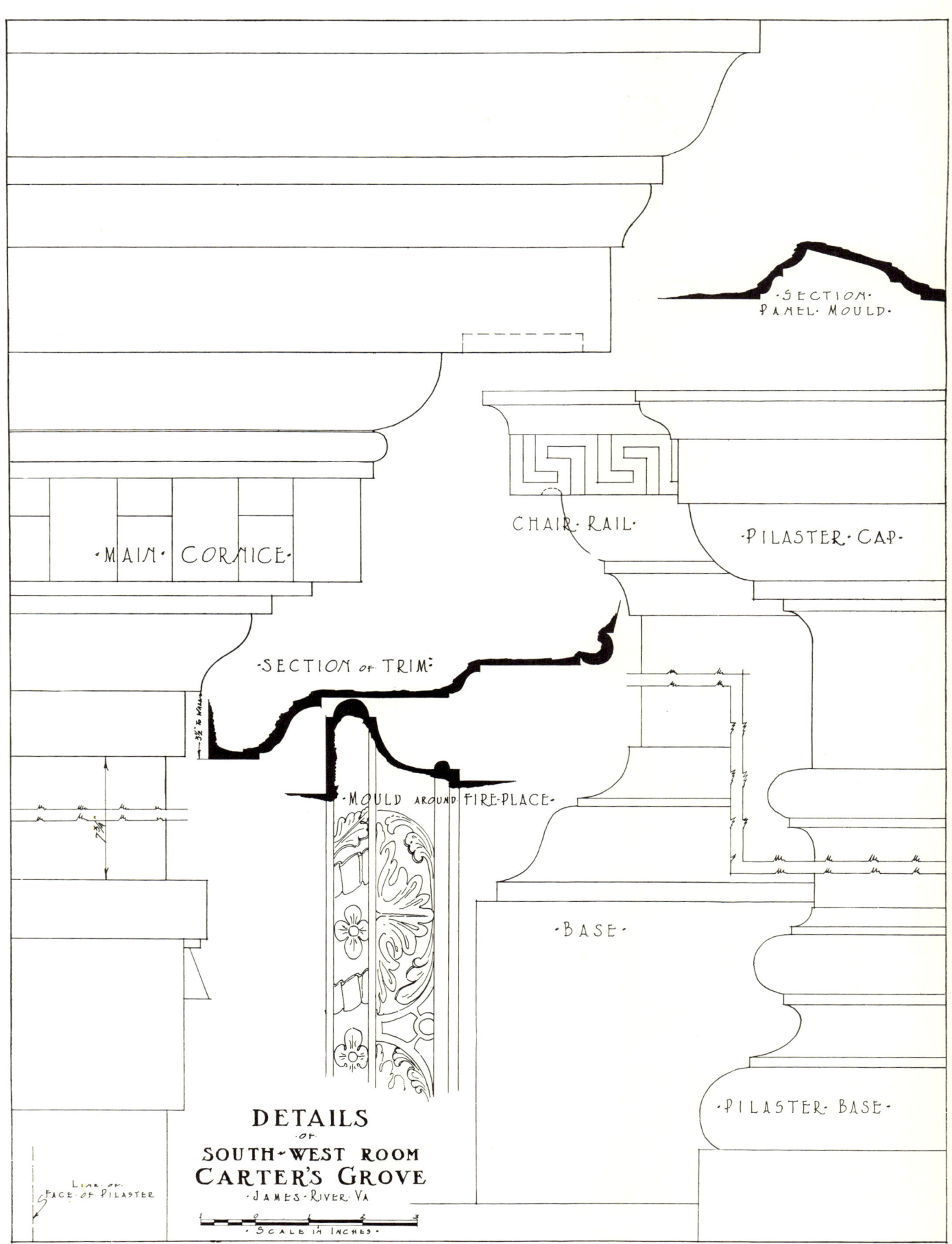

SHIRLEY, FROM THE GARDEN
CHARLES CITY COUNTY, VIRGINIA

EAST PORCH, SHIRLEY
CHARLES CITY COUNTY, VIRGINIA

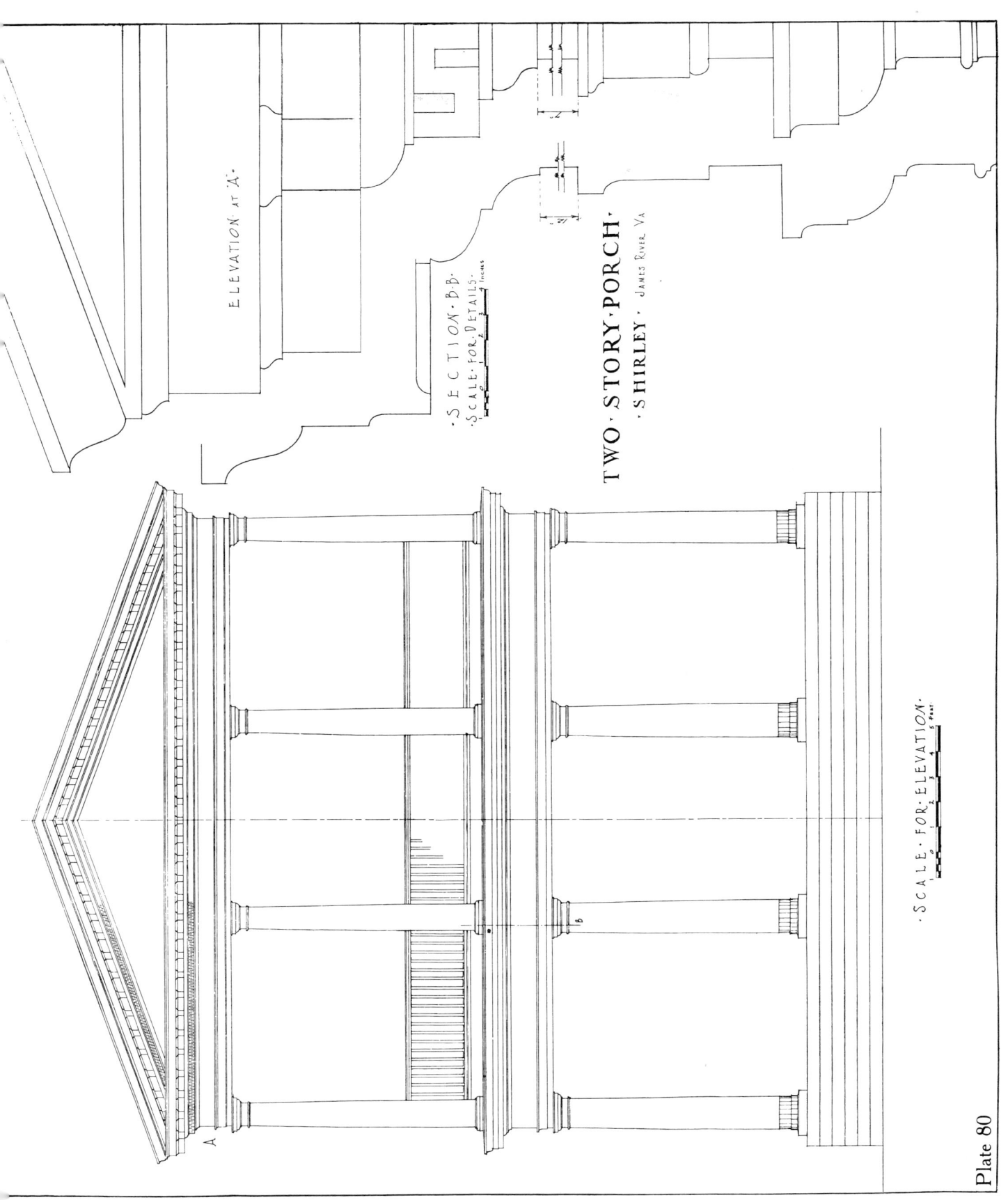

Plate 80

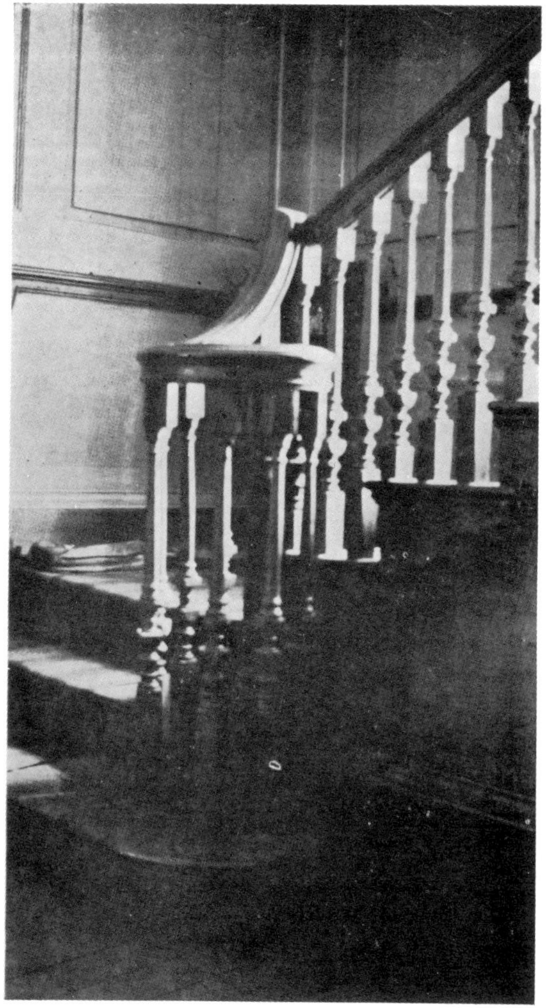

STAIR LANDING, SHIRLEY
CHARLES CITY COUNTY, VIRGINIA

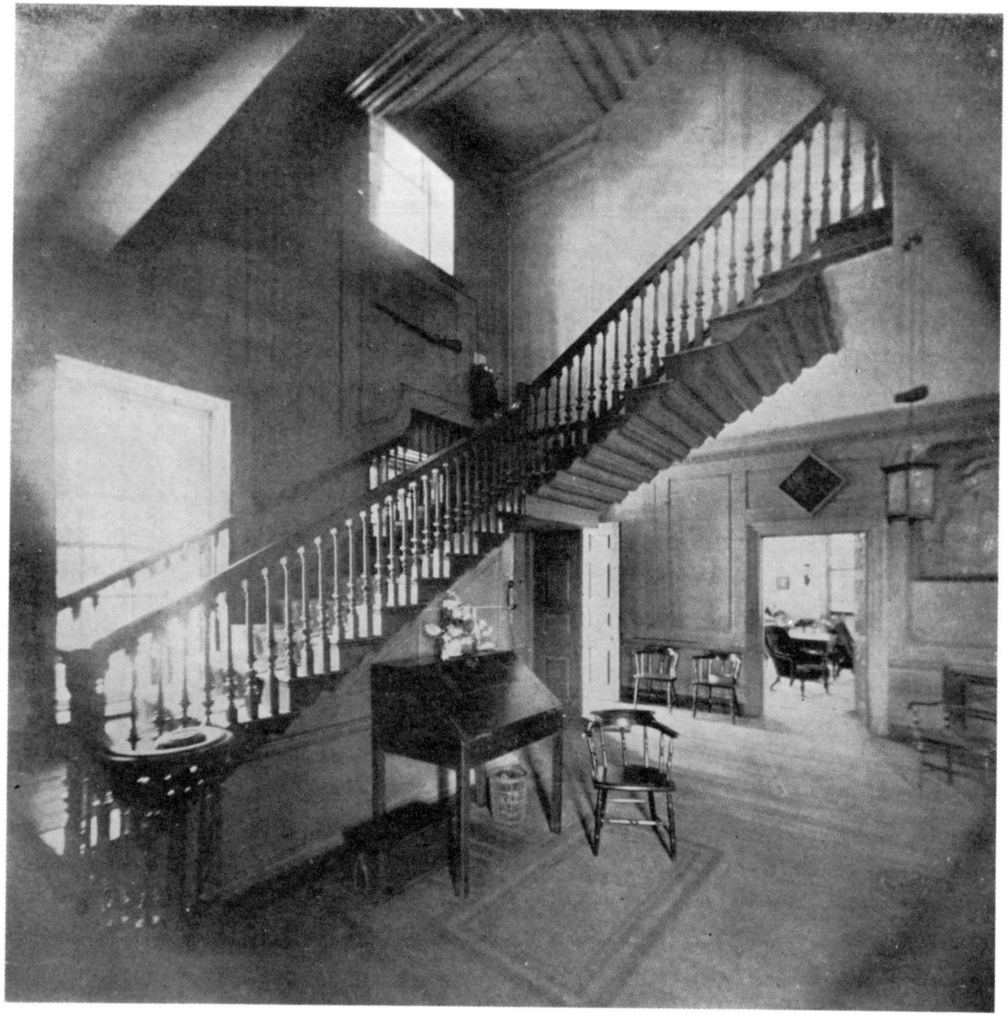

THE "HANGING STAIR" AND HALL, SHIRLEY
CHARLES CITY COUNTY, VIRGINIA

Plate 81

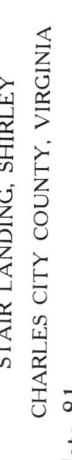

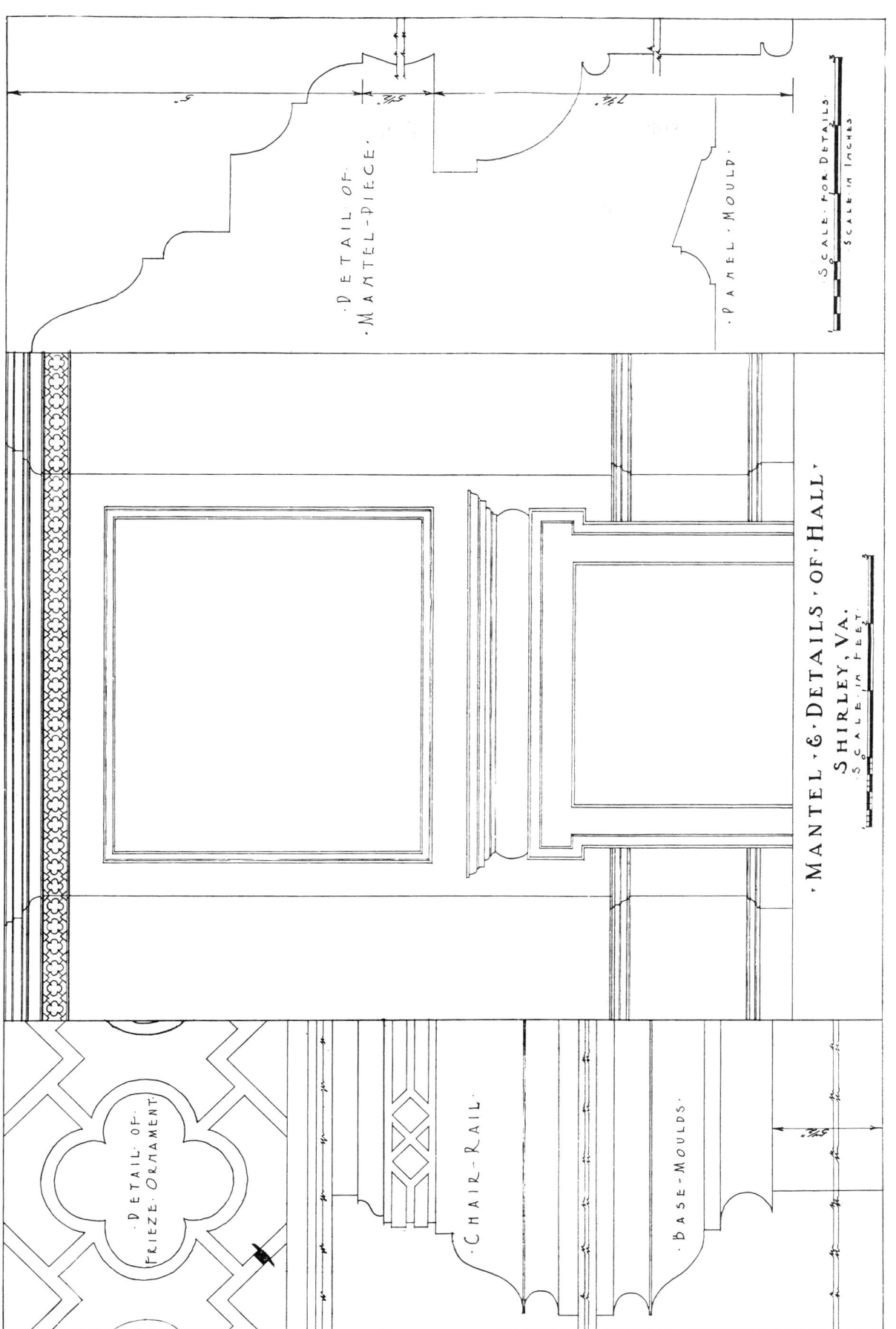

Plate 82

THE SALOON, SHIRLEY
CHARLES CITY COUNTY, VIRGINIA

Plate 83

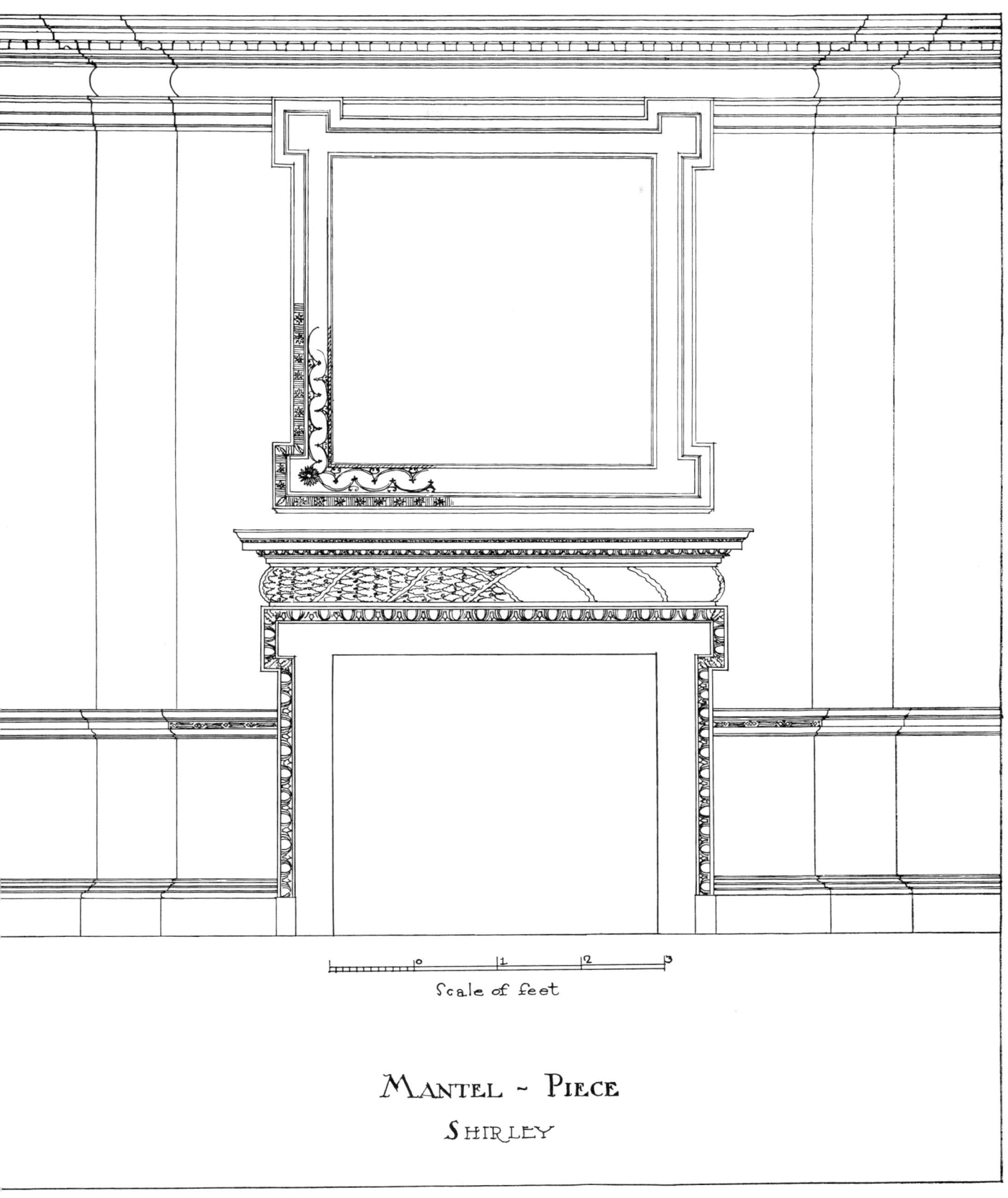

Scale of feet

MANTEL ~ PIECE

SHIRLEY

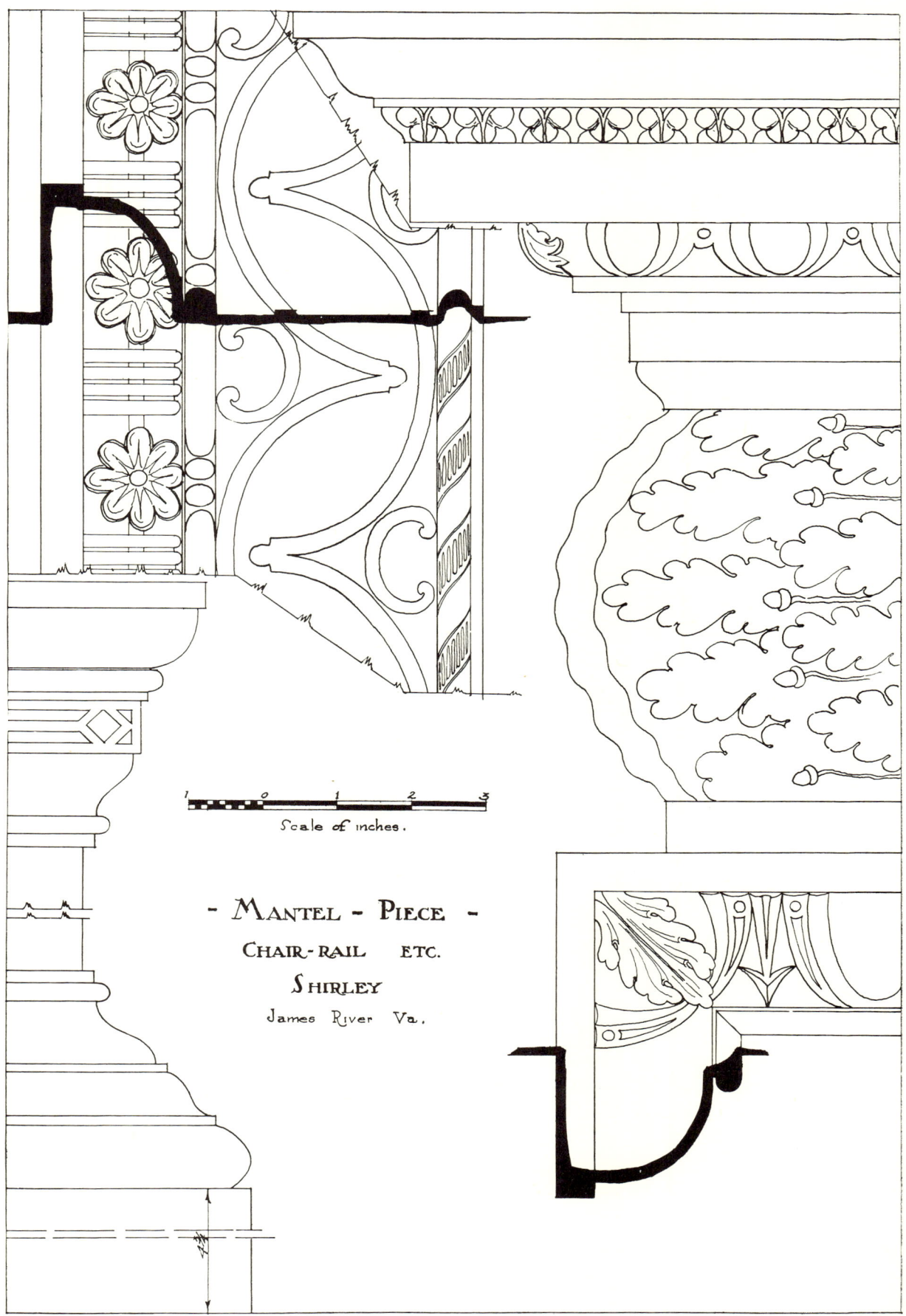

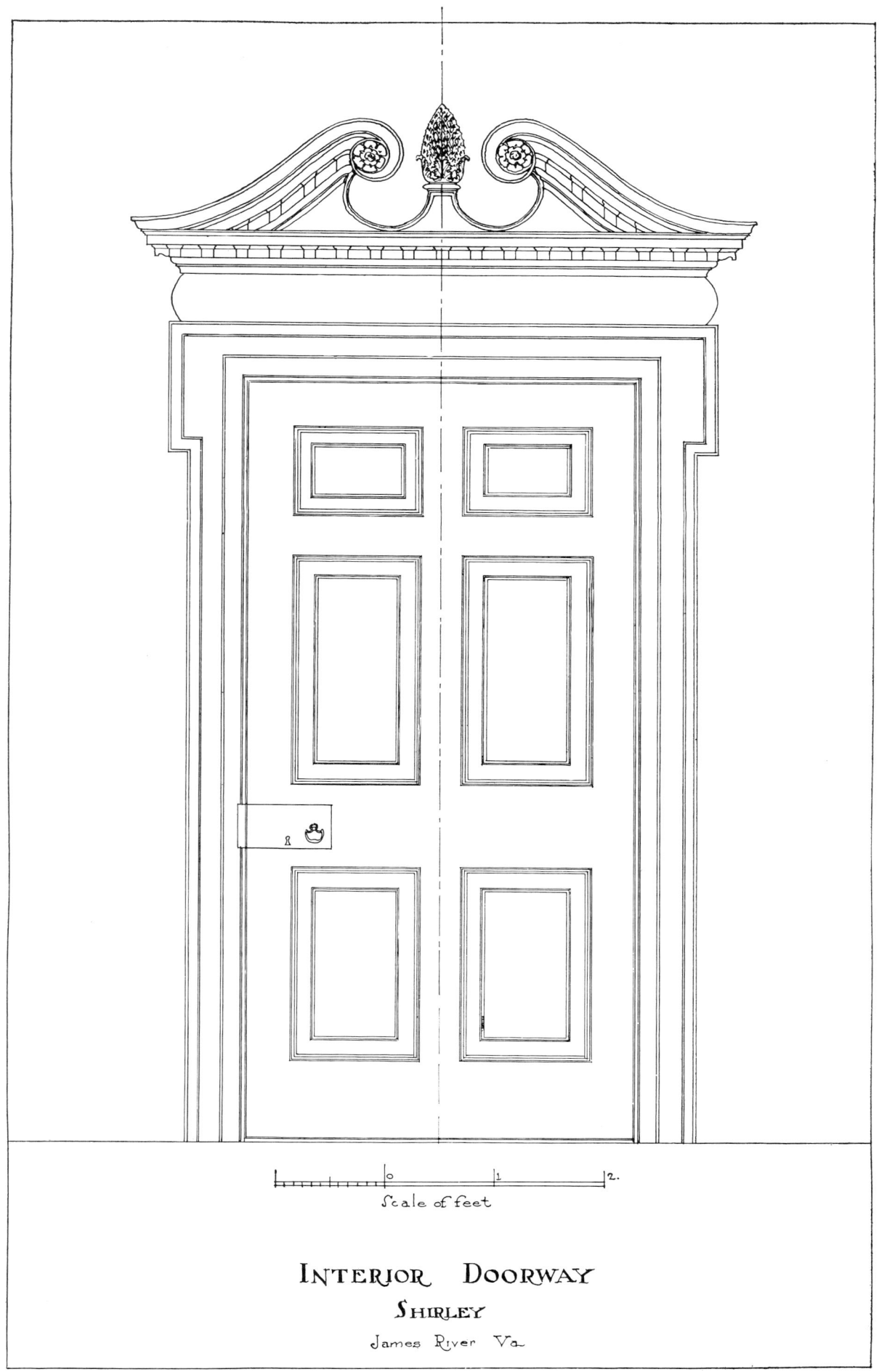

DETAIL FROM THE PARLOR, SHIRLEY
CHARLES CITY COUNTY, VIRGINIA

Plate 87

DETAIL FROM DINING ROOM, SHIRLEY
CHARLES CITY COUNTY, VIRGINIA

Plate 88

OLD DOVECOTE, SHIRLEY
CHARLES CITY COUNTY, VIRGINIA

Plate 90   FARM BUILDINGS, LOOKING TOWARD OFFICE, SHIRLEY
CHARLES CITY COUNTY, VIRGINIA

WESTOVER, 1727
CHARLES CITY COUNTY, VIRGINIA

Plate 91

DOORWAY, WESTOVER
CHARLES CITY COUNTY, VIRGINIA

GATE, WESTOVER
CHARLES CITY COUNTY, VIRGINIA

MAIN GATE, WESTOVER
CHARLES CITY COUNTY, VIRGINIA

Plate 92

THE ENTRANCE HALL, WESTOVER
CHARLES CITY COUNTY, VIRGINIA

Plate 93 DETAIL OF STAIRWAY, WESTOVER
CHARLES CITY COUNTY, VIRGINIA

LOWER BRANDON, FROM THE RIVER SIDE
PRINCE GEORGE COUNTY, VIRGINIA

Plate 94

THE ENTRANCE HALL, LOWER BRANDON
PRINCE GEORGE COUNTY, VIRGINIA

Plate 95   THE PARLOR, LOWER BRANDON
PRINCE GEORGE COUNTY, VIRGINIA

THE GARDEN, LOWER BRANDON
PRINCE GEORGE COUNTY, VIRGINIA

Plate 96

BACON'S CASTLE, 1660
SURRY COUNTY, VIRGINIA

MOUNT VERNON
FAIRFAX COUNTY, VIRGINIA

NELSON HOUSE
YORKTOWN, YORK COUNTY, VIRGINIA

OLD HOUSE IN YORKTOWN
YORK COUNTY, VIRGINIA

Plate 98

ROSEWELL, 1725 (DESTROYED)
GLOUCESTER COUNTY, VIRGINIA

Plate 99 THE GRAND STAIRCASE, ROSEWELL
GLOUCESTER COUNTY, VIRGINIA

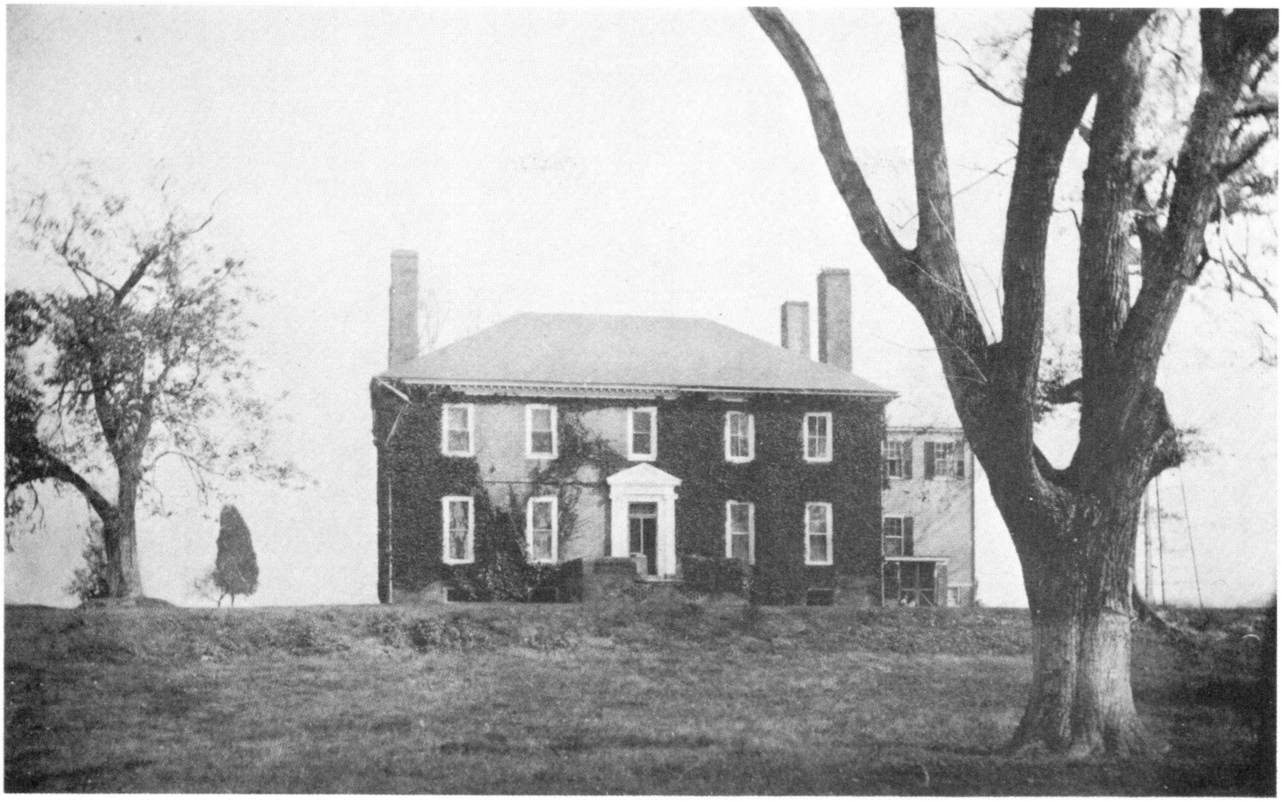

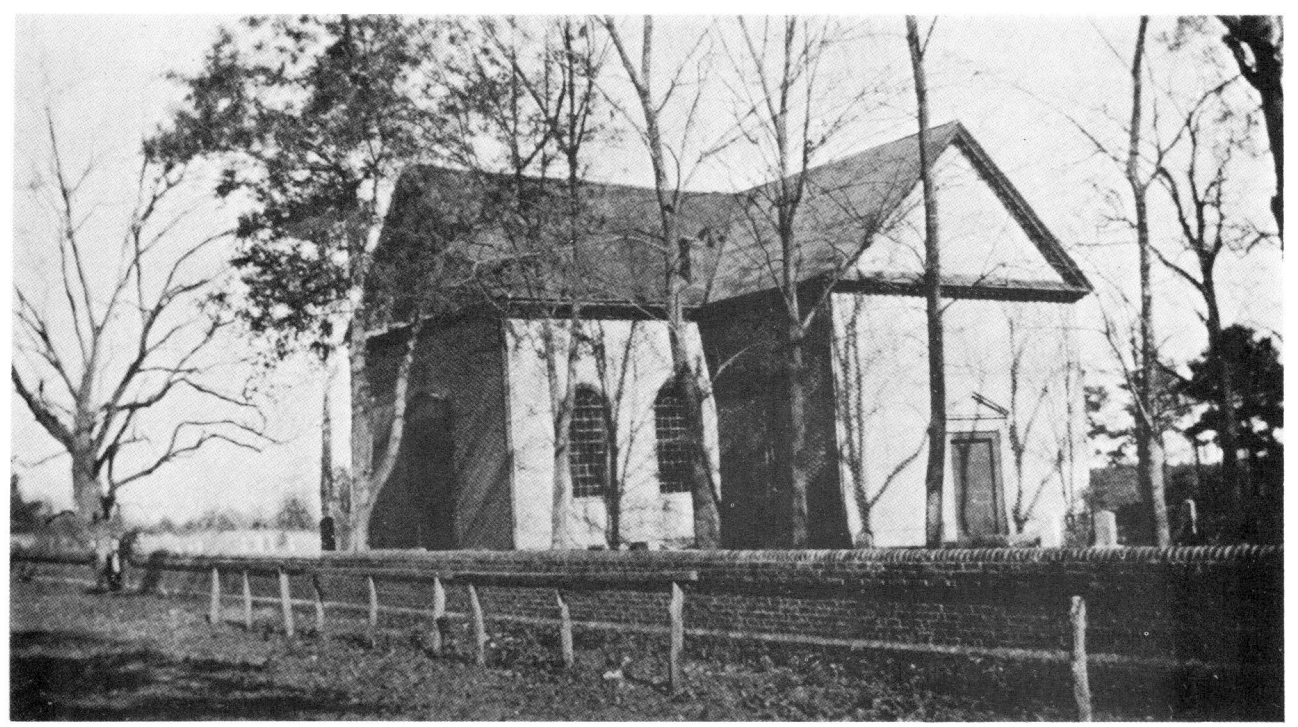

WILTON, FROM THE RIVER SIDE
HENRICO COUNTY, VIRGINIA

Plate 100

ABINGTON CHURCH
GLOUCESTER COUNTY, VIRGINIA

WEST DOOR, WILTON
HENRICO COUNTY, VIRGINIA

THE STAIRCASE, WILTON
HENRICO COUNTY, VIRGINIA

Plate 101

THE BOX GARDEN, TUCKAHOE
GOOCHLAND COUNTY, VIRGINIA

Plate 102

TUCKAHOE
GOOCHLAND COUNTY, VIRGINIA

Plate 103 THE SOUTH STAIRS, TUCKAHOE
GOOCHLAND COUNTY, VIRGINIA

MANTEL IN NORTHEAST ROOM, TUCKAHOE
GOOCHLAND COUNTY, VIRGINIA

Plate 104   THE NORTH STAIRS, TUCKAHOE
GOOCHLAND COUNTY, VIRGINIA

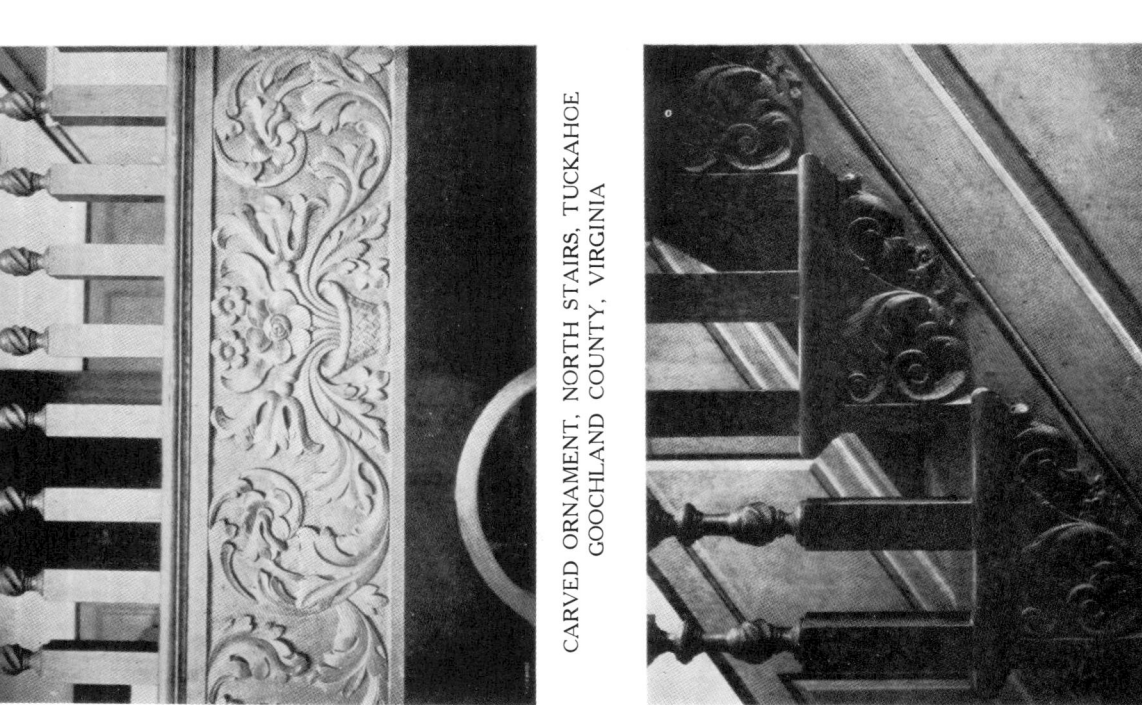

NEWEL, NORTH STAIRS, TUCKAHOE
GOOCHLAND COUNTY, VIRGINIA

CARVED ORNAMENT, NORTH STAIRS, TUCKAHOE
GOOCHLAND COUNTY, VIRGINIA

RISERS, THE NORTH STAIRS, TUCKAHOE
GOOCHLAND COUNTY, VIRGINIA

Plate 105

MYERS HOUSE
NORFOLK, VIRGINIA

Plate 106

THE LIBRARY, MYERS HOUSE
NORFOLK, VIRGINIA

Plate 107 MANTEL IN PARLOR, MYERS HOUSE
NORFOLK, VIRGINIA

MONTPELIER. (SHOWING RECONSTRUCTED WINGS)
ORANGE COUNTY, VIRGINIA

Plate 108

GIANT BOX, MONTPELIER
ORANGE COUNTY, VIRGINIA

Plate 109

THE GARDEN, MONTPELIER
ORANGE COUNTY, VIRGINIA

GARDEN FROM THE UPPER TERRACE, MONTPELIER
ORANGE COUNTY, VIRGINIA

ESTOUTEVILLE, 1830
ALBERMARLE COUNTY, VIRGINIA

Plate 111

GOOCHLAND COUNTY COURT HOUSE

Plate 112

THE ROTUNDA, FROM THE STREET
UNIVERSITY OF VIRGINIA, CHARLOTTESVILLE
ALBERMARLE COUNTY, VIRGINIA

ROTUNDA AND QUADRANGLE, FROM THE CAMPUS
UNIVERSITY OF VIRGINIA, CHARLOTTESVILLE, VIRGINIA

Plate 113

MONTICELLO, SOUTH PORTICO
ALBERMARLE COUNTY, VIRGINIA

Plate 114

NORTH PORTICO, MONTICELLO
ALBERMARLE COUNTY, VIRGINIA

Plate 115

THE WEST WING, MONTICELLO
ALBERMARLE COUNTY, VIRGINIA

THE MAIN HALL, MONTICELLO
ALBERMARLE COUNTY, VIRGINIA

Plate 116   THE RECEPTION ROOM, MONTICELLO
ALBERMARLE COUNTY, VIRGINIA

FARMINGTON
ALBERMARLE COUNTY, VIRGINIA

Plate 117

MANTEL IN PARLOR, TALLWOOD
ALBERMARLE COUNTY, VIRGINIA

BREMO
FLUVANNA COUNTY, VIRGINIA

Plate 118

BREMO, FROM THE RIVER SIDE
FLUVANNA COUNTY, VIRGINIA